I0094794

WILLY WAGTAIL

This edition published 2017
By Living Book Press
147 Durren Rd, Jilliby, 2259
Copyright © The Estate of C.K. Thompson, 1957

Cover photo by Duncan McCaskill.

The publisher would like to give a huge 'Thank You' to the author's family
for their assistance in making this book available once more.

All rights reserved. No part of this publication may be reproduced, stored in
a retrieval system, or transmitted in any other form or means – electronic, me-
chanical, photocopying, recording or otherwise, without the prior permission
of the copyright owner and the publisher or as provided by Australian law.

ISBN: 978-0-6481048-9-6

A catalogue record for this
book is available from the
National Library of Australia

WILLY WAGTAIL

By C.K. Thompson, R.A.O.U., J.P.

(Member of the Royal Australasian Ornithologists' Union)

CONTENTS

DEDICATION

To my good friend and fellow Honorary Magistrate, Mrs. ANNE J. TICKLE, J.P., of Waratah, N.S.W. in appreciation of her interest in the preservation of Australian wild life, and of her valuable assistance to me in the compilation of the Monthly News Bulletin of the Northern N.S.W. Federation of Justices of the Peace—an organisation of which I am the Founder, and of which I have had the honour to be President since its foundation.

FOREWORD

In most of the stories I have written about our Australian birds and animals, that friendly little chap, the black and white fantail, known affectionately to all of us as Willy Wagtail, has been one of the leading characters. I have found it almost impossible to write a book about our birds and fail to mention Willy. It was only natural, therefore, that, in due course, I should give him the title role in a story.

But this particular book was not intended to do that. Following a discussion with my publishers, it was agreed that I should write a book starring the Kookaburra, and when I started work, Old Jack did, in fact, have the centre of the stage. I had not proceeded far, however, before Willy Wagtail, the Bush Busybody, thrust his beak in, and eventually took over the leading role. The result was that I had to re-arrange the whole cast, and relegate Old Jack to second lead. I'll make it up to him some other time.

Regarding the descriptions of nest-stealing mentioned in this book, this habit among birds is world-wide. Experienced ornithologists have established that at least eighty different kinds of Australian birds appropriate the nests of other species. Most of them do so when the real owners have no further use for them; but there have been cases of forcible dispossession. Even Willy Wagtail has been guilty of it. He is reported to have used the open mud nest of a Welcome Swallow, and even that of his best friend, the Peewit or Mudlark. The latter's nest seems to be a great favourite among birds. As famous Australian ornithologist, Alec H. Chisholm, has written: "You can never be quite sure what kind of a bird you will see peering over the rim of a 'peewee's' old nest."

One last word about Willy. Is there an Australian who does not know the ubiquitous wagtail? Go where you will—in city park or garden, in suburban backyard, in the heart of the lonely bush—and there he is, the friend of all and the enemy of none. For Willy Wagtail is one of the most beloved and undoubtedly the most companionable little bird of all our interesting and unique wild life.

C. K. THOMPSON.

CHAPTER ONE
NESTING TIME

THE first touch of spring was upon the bushlands. In the early mornings the air was still tinged with the breath of Jack Frost, and after the sun went down the grey mists crept along the mountain gorges, arising from the placid creeks and waterholes. But as each day gave way to another, so did each grow longer and warmer.

In common with most other birds of their acquaintance, both friends and foes, Willy Wagtail and his mate were occupied in the very serious business of nest-building. Both were accomplished home architects, and the work was proceeding apace according to plans and specifications. They had selected the branch of a weeping willow tree that jutted out from the parent trunk above the waters of a deep, picturesque creek. It was an ideal nesting place, because the thick, graceful willow trailers provided an effective screen, behind which the little black-and-white birds had very good prospects of completing their home and rearing their chicks unmolested.

Willy and his mate had used various willow and gum trees along this creek for several seasons, and had raised quite a number of families. There had been losses, of course. On one occasion a heavy storm with gale-force winds had emptied the nest of three youngsters. The nest itself was too well constructed and too well attached to the limb to suffer damage. A second clutch of eggs had hatched and Willy and his mate had, in due season, launched a family into the world. There was one occasion when two eggs out of three were taken from the nest by a thieving small boy. The other had hatched out, but the nestling had provided a meal for a roving kookaburra.

But these were the ordinary ups and downs in the life of any bird, and Willy took them philosophically. Not that he could do much else; but he and his mate, during their short lives, had contributed, in no small measure, to the wagtail population of their particular district.

Taking all in all and this with that, their nesting area was a desirable locality in which food was always plentiful, and the existence of a farmhouse not far away provided the little birds with all the animal and human companionship they desired. Both were on very familiar terms with the farmer's horses and cows and had more than a nodding acquaintance with Farmer Campbell's family—especially his young son, Jimmy, who was a lad for whom they had very little use.

When completed, the wagtail's nest would be a thing of sheer beauty. Willy and his mate were natural architects, and knew how to construct their neat, cup-shaped home of strips of bark bound together with spider webs and held firmly in place on the horizontal branch with the same adhesive material. The bark could be had from any convenient tree, while the spiders that inhabited the barns and outhouses at the Campbell farm contributed lavishly of their webs. They did not do so voluntarily. Willy just took what he wanted without bothering about what the spiders thought of it. He was not interested in the spiders as food; he preferred flies and other small insects that he either snatched out of the air or trapped on leaves or on the ground.

But if Willy was not interested in spiders as food, his great friends and cronies the peewits or mudlarks were, and on several occasions that Willy went after webs, one or both of the peewits accompanied him—just for the meal.

Peewit and his mate had their nest in the same willow tree as Willy's, but on a higher limb. The four birds, similar in colouring, but so different in size, looks, habits and temperament, got along together in perfect harmony, and had often presented a united front to hawks, butcher birds, kookaburras and other nest robbers, including small boys. The four of them together made a very good fighting machine, while their united voices, loud and harsh, created a din enough to scare off many of their enemies, especially if those enemies had delicate eardrums.

Willy was only a little bird, but he had a complex nature. Not knowing the meaning of the word "timid," he was a very friendly little soul, ready to be matey with everyone. This, of course, did not include such deadly creatures as butcher birds, hawks and the like, cats—either native or tame—and the other predatory slayers who yearned to make a meal out of him and his family. Naturally he did not seek their friendship. All he wanted from them was to be left alone to live his own life in his own way.

One particular friend of Willy's was a large and placid old cow who provided the Campbell family with milk. Willy often used her as a convenient perch, riding on her broad back and employing her as a kind of bovine aircraft-carrier. She was generally surrounded by a halo of flies, and it was Willy's little habit to launch himself from her back among these flies, snap them up and return to the bovine flight-deck to consume his meal. The old cow also was an unconscious contributor to the lining of Willy's nest. His nestlings felt cosy and warm in their bed of soft cowhair.

As to the complexity of his nature—friendly and tame he was where domestic cattle and human beings were concerned; friendly he was where most other birds were concerned; but, being absolutely fearless, he often made a complete pest of himself, interfering in the private affairs of his feathered colleagues and frequently earning for himself a hiding that he did not always get. He was small, but he was swift, and so adept in aerial manoeuvring that there were few birds who could catch him. He was cunning enough never to get in the way of the arrow-swift falcons or the murderous butcher birds, but he was not averse at times to having a tilt at Old Jack Kookaburra. Old Jack was tough and hard and a killer too; but he was not much of a flier, a fact of which Willy took full advantage.

Unquestionably one of the greatest gossips in the bush, putting even those chatterers, the noisy miners or soldier birds, to shame on occasion, Willy was happy as long as he knew what was going on around the place. His mate was similarly inclined, but she hardly got a chirp in edgeways when Willy had the floor—or branch.

With nest-building in full swing, however, Willy did not have much leisure to loaf around the bush making a nuisance of himself with his inquisitive ways. One cannot mind other birds' business and carry out one's own efficiently at the same time.

As Willy got on with the nest-building job, he suddenly became conscious of the fact that things were not quite as they should be. Something seemed to be missing. There appeared to be a gap in the chain of events. The more he thought of it, the more he became concerned. Something, apparently, was going on somewhere and he was being kept out of it. This was an intolerable thought, so he decided to knock off work and try to find out what was what.

Perched on the branch at the side of the nearly-completed nest, Willy dabbed a piece of spider web into place with his small beak, and then took stock of his surroundings. First of all, the creek. Nothing out of the ordinary there—at least, it looked the same as usual. The willow tree was the same old tree he had known for years. The blue sky above was clear of feathered enemies and there were none that he could see in the tree itself, or on the banks, or on the surface of the water. A couple of redbills or waterhens were swimming near the reedy margin of the creek, but they were minding their own business. An open structure of rushes, leaves and grass placed on a platform of broken-down reeds showed that they were doing what Willy should have been doing—nest-erecting.

A sudden burst of "twitchee-twitchee-twitchee, quarty-quarty-quarty" from the thickets told Willy that a reed warbler was in residence. Willy saw these birds only in the nesting season. They spent the winter in the warmer regions far to the north, arriving at the creek around about August, and leaving again about March. A pair of spotted pardalotes or diamond birds were excavating a tunnel in the bank for their nest some distance down the creek, but they had been at that for some days now, as Willy knew. He missed nothing.

No, as far as he could see, all was as it should be around the creek.

In sudden decision, the little black-and-white bird took off and, looping upwards, landed on the branch that bore the peewits' nest. Peewit was engaged in poking bits of mud into position, but took time off to give Willy a brief, welcoming look. Then, having used his efficient beak as a trowel to slap the mud into a better shape, he fluffed out his feathers and gave a flat chirp. Willy replied with a loud "sweet pretty creature" which nearly shattered the peewit's eardrums. Giving Willy a reproachful look, the larger black-and-white bird flew down to the water's edge where its mate was poking around among the aquatic plants in search of her favourite food, pond snails. She seemed a little abashed by the arrival of her mate, for she immediately grabbed a beakful of mud and headed for the nest. Peewit did the same.

Willy was still on the branch near the large pudding basin-shaped mud nest, swinging his huge tail from side to side. He was more than a little taken aback when the female peewit greeted him with a stream of shocking language, which to his not very sensitive ear sounded something like this: "Listen to me, Willy Wagtail, if you have no work to do, you inquisitive little wretch, don't hold up birds who have. I saw you gabbing with that lazy mate of mine just now. Get back to your own limb and help your poor, over-worked hen. The trouble with you is, you talk too much and loaf too much, you little pest."

Of course, the peewit might not have meant that at all in her flat chatter, but it evidently aroused whatever Willy called his conscience, because he nose-dived straight down to his own limb, the nagging voice of Mrs. Peewit following him. And as he landed near his half-built nest, he knew what had been worrying him. His "poor, over-worked hen" indeed! Why, he hadn't seen the bird for hours! He had been fetching and carrying and doing all the work himself; that is, what work had been done, which was precious little.

With a chatter of anger, Willy darted into the air, half-looped and then shot off towards the farmhouse. It was there that he last remembered seeing her. They had both been collecting spider webs at the time. He had returned to the nest with a consignment, leaving her to follow. She hadn't.

CHAPTER TWO
WILLY MEETS A CAT

THE Campbell farm was mainly agricultural, with lucerne flats along the creek bank, and all types of vegetables in their season. The farmer owned a couple of cows, several plough and dray horses, a sty full of pigs, two dogs, a ginger cat and a number of fowls. He also possessed a wife, a pair of farm hands and a 12-years-old son, Jimmy. The farmhouse was large and rambling, with the usual collection of hay sheds, cowbails and assorted barns. It was around these outhouses that Willy and his mate collected the spider webs they used to bind their nest together.

When Willy reached the farm he alighted on a twig in a scraggy old peach tree. As the farmer never troubled to prune this tree, it was not a good bearer of fruit, the few that it did bring forth being shared by Jimmy and a host of codlin moth grubs. The tree was large and wild, but not too large or too wild to prevent Willy inspecting it within a minute or two. There was no sign of his missing mate. "Sweet pretty creature," said Willy, to nobody in particular.

"Sweet pretty creature," came an answering bird voice from the direction of the farmhouse. Willy swivelled around. It wasn't his mate's voice—in fact it did not sound much like a wagtail's call. Perched on top of the chimney was a biggish bird with glossy black plumage which had a metallic sheen. Its bill was pointed at the sky, and it was uttering wagtail calls, interspersed with sparrow chirps and silver-eye warbles.

Willy turned his back on the starling and its mimicking. He had little regard for imported pests, and starlings, though they were handsome enough in their way, were not native Australians. They were great destroyers of fruit and crops, even though they did eat a lot of harmful insects. They were very good mimics, as Willy knew, being able to imitate many different bird calls. Willy regarded this as sheer impertinence on the part of a bird whose ancestors came from Europe.

He swayed on the peach tree twig for a time while he surveyed the backyard of the farm. A few fowls were scratching fussily near the back door, watched sleepily by a large ginger cat lying on a bag on the doorstep. Willy knew this cat and it knew Willy. Neither had any love for each other. The wagtail had often flirted with sudden death by swooping down over the cat's back, chattering derisively as the animal made ineffectual swipes at it with its paws. Ginger did not like being made fun of, and if ever the cheeky Willy miscalculated a swoop, or relaxed his vigilance for one moment while on the ground, there would be a permanent merger of colours and black and white would be absorbed into ginger for evermore.

Ginger did not know that Willy was in the peach tree until the wagtail cut loose with a noise like peas rattling in a tin, followed immediately by his softer "sweet pretty creature." The sleepiness left Ginger's eyes and he flattened himself on the bag. Willy was sending out messages to his mate and did not notice the cat as it crept on its belly towards the tree. Reaching the bottom of the trunk, it gazed upwards with greedy, baleful eyes, and stretched out its front paws, getting a firm grip on the trunk with its claws.

But as it tensed itself for a spring that would send it some feet up the tree, Willy saw it. Swaying his big tail from side to side, he looked Ginger over appraisingly and then remarked, "Did-ja-did-jadid!" Ginger flattened back his ears at the harsh call, but did not move an inch. There was a branch only a few feet above him. Willy was six feet up past that and now that the element of surprise had gone, Ginger knew that he had no chance at all of catching the bird. Willy knew it, too, and his sweet pretty creature to the cat was arrogantly impudent.

With a deep, throaty growl, the cat sprang upwards, reaching the lower limb, his tail waving slowly. He glared at Willy, his teeth bared in a wicked snarl, while low rumblings in his throat indicated how dearly he would like to make a meal of the little bush nuisance, who had not shifted.

Willy hopped off his twig on to the parent limb, glanced downwards at Ginger six feet below, and then, catching sight of a passing insect, darted swiftly outwards, caught it and returned to his perch. Ginger, crouched on the limb below, would have to swarm several feet up the tree trunk to get at Willy, and Willy had no intention of allowing him to do that. But as long as it was safe to tantalise his feline enemy, he would do so.

Once again he directed a stream of uncomplimentary chatter at the cat and then, as if that were not enough, he suddenly made a dive at it, his little beak snapping within inches of the cat's head. Ginger, who had not expected that manoeuvre, was too late to do anything before Willy had returned to his former vantage point, but the sheer impudence of it stung him into movement. With a snarl, he ran up the tree trunk and reached the limb on which Willy was perched. Unconcernedly, the wagtail hopped up still higher, this time selecting a twig which would just bear his weight, but would certainly not hold that of a small kitten, let alone a full-grown cat.

Then Willy became positively overbearing. He chattered and he chirped, he dived into the air, looped the loop, flew backwards and forwards across the yard, made several circuits of the peach tree, took feinting dives towards Ginger and then returned to the twig again, swaying his huge tail from side to side so violently that it was a wonder he did not overbalance.

Crouched on the limb, Ginger glared at Willy with hate-filled eyes. The wagtail was only about a foot above him, but eight feet away. Ginger was near the trunk of the tree, while Willy was among the outermost leaves. He unconcernedly, and unnecessarily, preened one of his wings for a few seconds and then hopped down on to the limb on which Ginger crouched with hungry eyes and bristling whiskers.

The tomcat tensed for a spring, and Willy watched him warily. He then imitated half a box of matches being rattled—a vocal noise that irritated the cat beyond restraint. It sprang, but Willy was no longer on the limb. He was darting to and fro some feet above it like an intoxicated jet plane pilot.

Ginger squatted there and glared at him. The wagtail returned to the twig he previously had occupied and settled down to a thorough preening, keeping one eye on the movements of the enemy below. He broke off his toilet at one stage to advise Ginger that he was a "sweet pretty creature," an insincere compliment that the cat received in malevolent silence.

But somebody else did not receive it in silence. Mrs. Willy Wagtail, having returned to the nest in the willow and having found her mate missing, decided to look for him. She had not been loafing as Willy had thought. She had been on a hunt for material to line the nest away from the farmhouse; and that was why Willy had not found her there. Her arrival at the farm had coincided with her impudent mate's cynical compliment to Ginger.

Swooping down over the yard, she alighted on a clothesline and swayed there for a few moments while she searched the yard to locate Willy. That little pest, who had not seen her arrive, was still fooling around on his twig and tantalising the tomcat. But when he gave a sudden vocal exhibition of scissors-grinding like his cousin the restless flycatcher, Mrs. Willy pin-pointed him and flitted across to the peach tree.

It was sheer misfortune for the little bird that she was completely in ignorance of what had been going on in that peach tree. Had she announced her arrival by chirping or something, Willy could have given her warning. But she had not announced it.

From the clothesline she went darting down into the peach tree, alighting only a foot away from where the ginger cat crouched motionless. Ginger saw her and had her pinned down with a wicked, flashing paw before she had time to think.

But before the cat had time to act further, Willy was at him like a miniature fury. The gallant little bird, all his impudence and flirting forgotten, dived straight from his twig at the cat, his little beak snapping. He hurled himself between Ginger's eyes, the effect of the peck being equivalent to a match jabbed at a concrete wall. Whirling away and chattering harshly, he again flung himself at the cat, who lifted a paw to strike at him. Unfortunately for Mrs. Willy, it was not the paw that pinned her to the branch.

Without giving Ginger time to think, Willy flew at him again and again, pecking his head, his sides—in fact any part that presented itself. And as he did so his loud "did-ja-did-ja-did" rent the air. The row he kicked up attracted the attention of birds from far and near. His old friends the peewits, who had been eating grubs around the ploughed paddock, came flapping up together and added their grating cries to the general din. They flew in and out of the peach tree, while a flock of twittering sparrows, all sworn enemies of the ginger cat, strung themselves along the clothesline and chirped as loudly as they could. They did not go to Willy's assistance, but they urged him on vocally. So did a pair of Indian turtle doves who were nesting in the guttering of the Campbell farmhouse.

Like the sparrows and the starlings, they were, in Willy's opinion, foreign trash; but they were striking looking birds, those doves, with their grey heads, brown backs and wings, black necks with white spots, blackish tail feathers with white tips and cinnamon under-bodies. They threw a few sticks together in the guttering, called it a nest, laid two big white eggs and reared their pugnacious youngsters in poverty-stricken conditions. Argumentative also, replying to bird greetings with a call that sounded like a muttered "Is that so, huh?"

What with Willy Wagtail chattering, peewits squawking, sparrows chirping, doves cooing and hooting, roosters crowing and Ginger snarling, the combined uproar resembling a bush shire-council meeting, the peace of the farmyard was completely shattered. Open flew the back door, and out rushed young Jimmy Campbell.

"What's going on here?" he roared to the world in general.

Nobody had time to answer him. He saw the wild flutterings around the peach tree and ran to it, the better to investigate; and at that precise moment, one of the peewits and Willy himself hit Ginger at the same time. The peewit gave the cat a sharp peck on the head, while the wagtail got home a shrewd, painful peck right in the eye. It was too much for Ginger. He made a vicious slash with one paw and then with the other—and the captive hen wagtail fell to the ground at Jimmy Campbell's feet. She staggered upright, only to fall over again. Jimmy looked up in astonishment and then dropped his eyes to the wagtail moving feebly in the dust. He stooped and picked her up, just beating Ginger, who had come scurrying down the tree trunk, harried by Willy and the peewits, to try to retrieve his prize.

"I thought you wouldn't be far away," said Jimmy to Ginger. "So you had this waggie, did you? Well, get on your way, sailor, you're not having it for dinner this trip."

Saying which, the boy gave the cat a heavy kick in the ribs. Ginger spat in disgust and raced around the side of the house, while Willy and the peewits took refuge on the top of a shed, still voicing their opinions of cats. The sparrows had dispersed at the first appearance of Jimmy, but the doves still perched on the guttering, hooting and cooing.

"You look a bit used up," Jimmy remarked to Mrs. Willy, who lay in the palm of his hand, moving feebly. "But you ain't dead, anyway. I'll shove you in a box until you recover and then you can push off. Let Ginger clean up the useless sparrows if he wants a bird feed."

"Zat so, huh?" cooed a dove from the roof.

"Yep, that's so," retorted Jimmy. "And I'll be up there soon cleaning that nest of yours out of the guttering. Every time it rains the gutter flows over with the muck you've shoved in it."

Jimmy Campbell unearthed a rusty old canary cage and gently placed Mrs. Willy on the floor in it. Then he hung the cage on a nail at the side of the fowlhouse, high enough to prevent Ginger getting at it. That done, he stood and watched for a while. Mrs. Willy, apart from the loss of a few feathers, had not been hurt bodily, but she had suffered a big shock as well as having had the wind knocked out of her by the tomcat's ungentle paw. Ginger had had no time to get her into his mouth, otherwise the story would have had a different ending.

A rasping noise from directly above him drew Jimmy's eyes upwards. On the edge of the fowlhouse roof sat Willy Wagtail, swaying gently backwards and forwards and peering down anxiously.

"Ah, there, old timer," greeted Jimmy. "Is this a pal of yours in this cage? Your missus, maybe, huh?"

"Sweet pretty creature," said Willy.

"Every time I see myself in the mirror I say that, Willy," chuckled Jimmy. "However, I suppose you want to talk it over with the old girl, no? Maybe I'd better leave the cage door open so that you can visit the hospital ward and give her a bunch of flowers, huh?"

"Did-ja-did-ja-did!" grated Willy.

"Don't hurry me, I'll fix it," said the boy. Searching around, he found a bit of string and with this he secured the cage door so that it would remain open. Then he waved his hand to Willy and retired to the peach tree, against which he leaned his back, the better to watch developments.

Willy stayed on the edge of the fowlhouse roof for some minutes, swaying his big tail to and fro and keeping a wary eye on Jimmy. He neither liked nor trusted the boy and momentarily expected him to start something detrimental to his wagtail welfare. The peach tree was fifty feet or so away from the fowlhouse.

Willy, though bold and impudent, could also be very cautious. He sensed some kind of a trap here. Although his small mate was only a few feet below him, she was surrounded by something that was as unattractive as it could be menacing.

It was a feeble chirping noise from the cage that made him move. The little hen bird was crouched in a corner, unhurt, but not feeling the best. Willy left the fowlhouse roof and darted backwards and forwards in front of the cage several times, chirping in a low tone. His mate replied weakly. Willy then made a complete circuit of the yard, closely examining it and pin-pointing each living object. There was no sign of the cat, the fowls were going about their ordinary business, the sparrows were scuffling in the dust, and the doves, the starling and his friends the peewits had vanished. Only Jimmy Campbell remained, leaning against the peach tree like a toppling statue.

Reassured, Willy decided to take a chance. He darted straight at the cage and perched on top of it. Peering through the rusty wires, he chattered to his mate inside. She made a feeble leap from the floor to the single perch, wobbled unsteadily and fell off. Willy left the cage roof, half-looped and then clung to the front wires. Cocking his head around the open door, he chirped "sweet pretty creature." Mrs. Willy looked at him droopy-eyed, opened and closed her beak a few times as if she were very bored, but said nothing. Willy hopped through the open doorway and joined her, nuzzling her with his small beak. She returned the endearment.

"Why don't you kiss her?" shouted Jimmy Campbell from the peach tree. Startled, Willy shot through the doorway, looped upwards and came to rest again on top of the fowlhouse. Surprised at his sudden departure, Mrs. Willy hopped to the doorway and looked out. Harshly, Willy told her to join him, but she merely sat there. Impatiently, Willy again dived down and clung to the side wires near the door. His "sweet pretty creature" was an urgent plea for her to stir herself and let them both get away from this place. Willy didn't like it. He sensed danger. As long as he was in the region of that cat and that boy, he was uneasy.

Several times he flew from the cage to the fowlhouse and back again, sometimes perching on the cage top, sometimes clinging to the side or front wires, but never entering the cage itself. Occasionally he varied the performance by looping the loop, but he could not make his mate leave the cage. The fact was, Mrs. Willy had not quite recovered from her shock, but was regaining strength steadily.

It was when Willy became really angry in his anxiety, and threatened to attack his mate, that Jimmy Campbell interfered. He walked towards the cage, clapping his hands in an endeavour to scare Mrs. Willy into the open. Willy saw him coming and his rage towards his mate turned towards this human intruder. Boldly he made a dive at Jimmy, his little beak snapping over the boy's head. Jimmy made an involuntary smack at Willy but missed him. Mrs. Willy became excited and while Willy was dive-bombing Jimmy, she took her courage in both wings, left the cage doorway, and managed to wobble her way up to the fowlhouse roof. Willy saw her, screeched his delight, and flew swiftly to her side.

Several times he took to the air and flitted off, only to return to urge her to follow him. And at last she did. She took to the air and made her staggering way across the paddocks, closely shepherded by Willy, who circled her continuously as if to ward off any attackers. But there were none, and the pair of small birds eventually reached their willow tree. Mrs. Willy dropped into the half-built nest to finish her convalescence. Willy fussed around her, perching on the limb and "sweet pretty creaturing" like a screen-struck nurse at the bedside of a famous movie star.

Back at the farm, Jimmy Campbell rubbed his hands in satisfaction.

"I feel like a Boy Scout. I've done my good deed for the day," he remarked to Ginger, who had emerged, sulkily, from underneath the house. Ginger, tail and nose in the air, walked past him in utter disdain, ignoring him completely.

CHAPTER THREE
JIMMY MEETS NEMESIS

JIMMY Campbell and his three chosen mates sat side by side on the bank of the creek and idly dangled their bare feet into the placid water while they discussed the best method of spending that particular Saturday.

There was much in common and much at variance among the four lads. They were all of the same age, they all nearly ruined their parents by the way they treated their clothes, they were all tousle-headed, they all, with one exception, had plenty of freckles, they all attended the same school and drove the same teacher to the verge of insanity, and they all possessed nicknames.

Jimmy was the self-elected chief of the gang and the others tolerated that leadership unless it interfered too much with their own strong inclinations; for each of the boys had a will of his own and could stand up for his own rights.

Young Campbell had been christened James Angus, but his young friends had re-christened him "Humpy." They had done this by the involved line of thought that seemed to govern the selection of many nicknames. His name was Campbell.

Campbell was a name like "camel." A camel had a hump. Therefore, Jimmy became "Humpy." His ancestors came from the Scottish Highlands, but Jimmy knew practically nothing about Scotland and cared even less.

Diametrically opposed to him in that particular regard was young Ian Donald Macdonald, a sandy-haired youngster whose ancestors also had come from the Highlands. Ian was intensely proud of his Scottish forebears and sometimes made an utter bore of himself in that regard. He knew more about the histories of the Scottish clans than he did about the history of his native Australia. He was a bore even to his father, who had come to Australia as a small boy with his parents.

It was young Ian Macdonald who reduced a very small lassie to tears at a Robert Burns Night concert by loudly informing her that a kilt was male attire and should never be worn by a woman; and that in no circumstances whatsoever should a woman wear a sporran. As the small lassie wore both, it was, in Ian's eyes, a double crime of the deepest dye. She had been billed to do a Highland Fling on the stage, but after young Mr. Macdonald had concluded his lecture, she was fit for nothing but weeping, which she did loudly and wetly. This drew her mother into the conversation and when that good lady had finished addressing the meeting, Ian's father took him by the ear, led him to the door, gave him a lift under that ear and told him to go home before the whole of the clans represented at the concert took to him.

Ian's nickname of "Scotty" was, in the circumstances, most appropriate.

Eric Birch, the third of the quartet, was a young gentleman of a somewhat studious turn of mind, whose main diversion was reading books of all kinds. A treatise on rock formations in the Swiss Alps received from him the same earnest attention as a blood-curdling novel of Australian bushrangers. He could find romance in a railway timetable and virtue in a school geography book. This queerness on his part did not commend him to his little friends, but Mr. Birch could use his fists as well as the rest of them. For that they respected him and tolerated his touch of book-reading insanity. His pet name was "Tiger," possibly because he looked more like a belligerent mouse than the striped terror of the Indian jungle.

Last of the company was a lad who appeared to be strangely out of place among that company, quite apart from the fact that he alone of them all had no freckles on his face. A New Australian lad from Poland, he had a name that none of them could pronounce properly. They did not try to do so.

They got over the obstacle by christening him "Egghead." This, in spite of the fact that his head in no way resembled an egg.

Egghead had come to Australia as a very small child and his English was as good as theirs, better in fact. He did not employ all the slang they did. He was intelligent and quick to learn. He could use a catapult expertly, he knew all the loose palings in the fences of all the district orchards, he could stand up to anyone his own size (and bigger) in a fist fight, and he was devoted to Tiger Birch. Tiger was his best friend and idol, a thing that always puzzled Scotty and Humpy, who regarded Tiger as very ordinary potatoes, as well as being just a trifle mad. This madness was caused, obviously, by too much knowledge and the unnatural pursuit of more. Added to which, Tiger was continually lecturing Egghead on the shortcomings of New Australians in general and their predilection for killing all kinds of native birds to eat.

"Well," said Humpy Campbell impatiently, "none of you blokes have come forward with any bright ideas on how we are gonna spend today. I'm sick of fishing, so don't suggest that, you mugs."

"We'll go fishing if we feel like it, Humpy," snorted Scotty. "Say we all go and..." began Tiger, but Humpy cut him short.

"That's out, too," he said rudely.

"Dash it, I didn't say what I was going to, you ignorant coot," protested Tiger.

"You didn't have to. All your ideas are nutty," said Humpy.

"You're not so hot yourself, Humpy," snorted Tiger warmly.

"We could walk in the forest and collect the eggs of birds," suggested Egghead. "This is the nesting time of spring."

"We know that without you telling us, Egghead," said Humpy. "That's out. Too much trouble scaling trees."

"Apart from which, nobody should go robbing birds' nests," said Tiger. "That's you New Australians all over. Don't you realise that many species of birds have died out because of people pinching all their eggs—not only New Australians either. The old ones are worse."

"What of it?" demanded Humpy. "Who cares about that?"

"I do, for one," said Tiger.

"If we collected eggs, we would take just one from each nest. That would not kill them all off," said Egghead. "And New Australians do not steal birds' eggs. Some of them have shot kookaburras to eat not knowing that it is wrong. They are very sorry for it."

"Yes, the police see to that," said Humpy. "Anyway, you blokes can go ahead if you like. Not me. What about you, Scotty?"

"Nothing doing," replied that young man. "I think I'll have a dip in the creek."

"And that's something you can have all on your own,

too," shuddered Tiger. "The water is too cold. I'm waiting for summer."

"Sissy!" said Scotty insultingly, but Tiger was unmoved.

"Hey, what about us playing follow-the-leader?" exclaimed Humpy. "We haven't played that for a long time. I'll lead, and you coves have to follow me no matter where I go."

The others looked at him without enthusiasm, but with great suspicion. They had played that game before with Humpy Campbell leading, and they had landed into all sorts of unpleasantness.

"Well, how about it?" said Humpy impatiently. "Are you blokes too chicken-hearted or something? Are you scared I might dive into the creek and swim across, or eat a handful of mud or something?"

"I wouldn't put anything past you, Humpy," said Scotty candidly. "We have all had experience of you and your follow-the-leader. Play it on your own."

"I bet you I can cross this creek without getting my feet wet," challenged Humpy. "If I can, will you follow me?"

That made them more suspicious than ever. The creek was about 20 feet wide here, and they knew that Humpy could not jump it. There were no boats, and, as far as they could see, no logs on which he could walk across or float across, and no debris out of which he could build a raft.

"How will you do it?" inquired Egghead.

"By climbing that old willow tree, swinging on to the limb of that gum tree up there, and scaling down the trunk on the other side."

"You mean, failing down and breaking your silly neck, don't you?" grunted Tiger.

"I'll give it a go, anyway. What is more, I don't care whether you sissies follow me or not."

"Go ahead, Humpy. After all, it's your own neck,"

shrugged Scotty.

Jimmy Campbell walked to the foot of the willow tree and measured it with his eye. It sloped slightly out over the creek and was easy climbing to an expert like him. Conveniently jutting boughs assisted him greatly, and he made good time.

Hauling himself on to a large branch, he paused for a few seconds and had a look around. It was then that he sighted Willy Wagtail's nest a few feet along the limb. Mrs. Willy was on the nest and under her were three yellow-brown eggs with dark markings.

Mrs. Willy looked at Jimmy warily.

"Sweet pretty creature," said Humpy ingratiatingly. Mrs. Willy said nothing, but her wariness increased.

"Did-ja-did-ja-did-ja-did!" croaked Humpy.

"What the dickens are you talking about up there?" shouted Tiger Birch from the ground.

"I'm making love to a lady wagtail in a nest up here, but she won't be in it," shouted Humpy in return.

"You can't blame her for that," bawled Tiger.

"Tell Egghead he can climb up and collect the googies if he wants them," Humpy called down. "I'm now gonna scale up to another branch before I can swing over to the gum tree."

The three boys below and the wagtail on the nest watched his progress with interest. He reached the desired limb and was crawling slowly along it when they saw him pause. In front of him was the peewits' nest, untenanted for the moment, but containing four reddish-white spotted eggs.

"Stone the crows," Humpy yelled to his watching mates. "This joint is like a guesthouse. You can't move for blessed birds' nests. Here's a mudlark's with four googies in it."

"Well, leave it alone," shouted Tiger, gawking upwards with open mouth.

Grinning to himself, Humpy carefully lifted one of the large eggs from the mud nest and poised it, taking careful aim at Tiger. That lad, still gazing upwards with wide-open mouth, was greatly taken aback when the egg dropped cleanly and neatly into it!

To say that Tiger was surprised would be grossly to understate it. His eyes bulged from their sockets, he made choking and spluttering sounds and his face took on the hue of a boiled beetroot. Bending his head and grasping his stomach with both hands, he spat and gurgled and it was touch and go whether he swallowed the peewit omelette or managed to eject it.

He received no assistance or sympathy from his little playmates. Scotty Macdonald was staggering around and screaming hysterically, while the less demonstrative Egghead was grinning all over his face and rubbing his hands together in delight. Up in the tree, Humpy Campbell was clinging to the branch, nearly suffocated with laughter.

With a supreme effort, Tiger managed to spit out some of the egg-and-shell mixture, but he had swallowed most of it. It was lucky for him that the egg had been laid only a few days previously, otherwise it would not have been at all to his taste. Leaning against the tree trunk, his face mottled and his forehead bedewed with perspiration, he surveyed his howling friends with rage in his heart.

"All right, you can laugh, you stupid lot of half-boiled rat bags," he shouted; and then resumed his spitting and spluttering.

"W-we're d-doing our b-best to, Tiger," gurgled Scotty. "W-what price eggs for b-breakfast? Haw! haw! haw!"

"Ha, ha, ha!" came a roar of mirth from up the willow tree. "You'll be the death of me yet with your jokes, Tiger!"

"Come down out of that dashed tree, Humpy!" roared

Tiger fiercely. "I'll murder you, you—you—!" Words failed him.

"And you're the bloke who told Egghead not to go robbing nests," laughed Scotty. "Old Egghead doesn't eat birds' eggs anyway! We'll have to call you Eggeater to match him."

"Haw, haw, haw, that's a good 'un," came drifting down from the tree. "Eggeater Birch, the terror of the bush. Won't the mob at school give you what-for when they hear about this:—." Humpy broke off suddenly and yelled, "Hey, clear off, you mugs... shoo! shoo!"

Looking upwards, the boys on the creek bank saw young Mr. Campbell clinging to the branch with one arm while he made rapid passes with the other at two indignant peewits. The excited birds were circling him and diving at his head, chattering their dislike. They had both been away feeding on pond snails further up the creek and had returned to their nest to find this human interloper interfering with it.

Down below, Mrs. Willy Wagtail, who had sat tight on her nest throughout the whole of the prior proceedings, felt that she must be in on this lot. Being a wagtail, she had to shove her beak in. She flitted upwards, arriving at the scene of hostilities just as Willy himself turned up. That little busybody had been over in the farm paddock riding around on the back of his old friend the cow when, hearing the distant racket kicked up by the peewits, he had returned like a black-and-white rocket. Seeing Jimmy Campbell, the boy for whom he had but little use, he threw himself into the fray with glee.

Humpy Campbell now received the combined attention of four irate birds. The peewits were four times the size of the wagtails, and had much more efficient beaks for wreaking dreadful vengeance on a marauder the size of Humpy. They also had wings and they used them, buffeting the boy about the head and face while Willy and his mate did the same, all getting in each other's way and confusing the issue.

Had Humpy been possessed of cast-iron nerves and had been content just to cling to the branch with both hands, he may not have come to a great deal of harm. A few scratches from claws or beaks would no doubt have been the full extent of his injuries before the birds got tired of it and left him alone. But Humpy became greatly confused and each time he felt a wing brushing his face or heard a harsh voice in his ear, he instinctively made a wild smack at the air.

It was when one of the peewits managed to give him a sharp peck on the nose that disaster befell him. The peck hurt, and it caused Humpy to let go the branch and clasp both hands to his nose. The inevitable happened. There was a loud roar, a great tearing of leaves and twigs, culminating in a terrific splash as young Mr. Campbell hit the surface of the creek fifteen feet below and vanished from sight.

"Gosh! Humpy's fallen into the creek!" shouted Scotty, stating the obvious.

"Serve him right. I hope the fool drowns," snorted Tiger vindictively.

"He won't," said Egghead.

He didn't, for as the three boys stood on the bank and eagerly gazed at the turbulent surface of the creek, Humpy's head popped into view. The water in that spot was no more than six feet deep, and Humpy, like all of them, was an accomplished swimmer. His appearance caused much unfeeling laughter among his friends, who made no attempt to assist him up the bank. Loudest laughter came from Tiger Birch, who felt that justice had been done; that Nemesis had overtaken Humpy and that he deserved all he got.

"Nice weather for ducks," he remarked with a grin.

Humpy did not reply to that. He waded to the bank and

as he did so, Scotty made a weird noise which he fondly thought resembled bagpipes and then shouted the war song of Humpy's ancestors:—

"The Campbells are coming, hurrah, hurrah!"

Humpy ignored him. He reached the bank, hauled himself to dry land and stood there glowering and shivering. The day was sunny but not very warm and he felt a trifle chilly in his wet and muddy clothes.

"What made you jump into the creek, you silly fellow?" asked Egghead when the laughter had died down. "I am glad that we did not agree to play follow-the-leader with you. Fancy diving into the creek on a day like this! You said you were going to cross the creek on the trees."

"Look, do you blokes think I dived into that creek on purpose?" exclaimed Humpy. "If you really want to know, I got pushed into it by a pair of dashed mudlarks and a pair of confounded wagtails."

That statement caused a renewed gale of laughter and chaffing, which irritated Humpy beyond measure and turned his thoughts to murder. He informed his friends that they were deficient in brains and if there was any more funny stuff, he'd throw the three of them into the creek. They asked him where he thought he could get a dozen strong men in a hurry to help him.

While this argument had been in progress, the triumphant birds had settled down in the willow above. Mesdames Peewit and Wagtail resumed incubation on their respective nests, while Mr. Peewit stood on guard. Willy Wagtail flew down unobserved and perched on the top of an old stump not far away from the wrangling boys. He was interested in them.

"Well, I'm not going to stay here and freeze to death," grunted Humpy. "I'm gonna gather up some dry wood and make a fire. I'm all wet and as cold as billy-oh. You coves gonna help me?" The coves kindly agreed to assist and began to search around for twigs and bark. Then it was discovered that none of them possessed any matches.

"Fat lot of good you jokers are," growled the shivering Humpy. "I'm going home to change. I'll see you some more."

"Watch out that some more wagtails don't push you back into the creek," jibed Tiger Birch. "I ought to belt your ears off for dropping that peewit's egg into my mouth, but I'll let you off this time, seeing that the peewits paid you out by heaving you into the drink."

"Look, Tiger, I'll bash your brains in for that!" exclaimed Humpy savagely.

"Sweet pretty creature," interjected Willy from the stump.

"And I'll bash your brains in first," howled Humpy, picking up a stick and whirling around. He sent it flying through the air like a boomerang and it whizzed right under Willy's beak. With a screech of alarm, Willy took to the air and fled wildly across country, taking refuge in a grove of banksias a fair distance away.

Humpy grunted. He did not resume hostilities towards Tiger, but turned on his heel and squelched wetly away without a further word.

"What do we do now?" inquired Scotty. "How about a stroll over into the bush? We might get some sport with our catapults."

"Or collect some birds' eggs," said Egghead eagerly.

"There is no need, as I've said time and time again to you fellows, to go about destroying birds and their eggs. You never see me shooting them with a catapult," said Tiger.

"No. I suppose you carry it around to shoot butterflies with," said Scotty sarcastically.

"I am willing to have a walk in the bush," said Egghead.

"That is, if Tiger is," he added, looking expectantly at his hero.

"Okay, then, let's go," said Tiger.

CHAPTER FOUR
OLD JACK KOOKABURRA

PERCHED on a limb of an ironbark growing on the highest crest of the hill, Old Jack Kookaburra surveyed the countryside and approved of it. The sun was half-way up the eastern sky, and lying upon a fleecy white cloud it threw a warming light over the majestic grandeur of the distant mountains. It glittered on the fringe of bush that clothed the lower slopes and turned the leaves into flakes of green gold.

To the north, the open bush was a sea of emerald. To the south, Old Jack could see the irregular line of bright green cut with silver that marked the willow-edged creek which was the home of Willy Wagtail and his peewit friends.

All around him the bush was a hive of industry as birds, both large and small, built nests, laid eggs, hatched them or fed their chicks. Old Jack should have been on the job himself. Instead of loafing on that limb, he should have been searching around for a nesting place in a hollow limb, a hole in a tree or a termites' nest to excavate. Last season he and his mate had occupied a termites' nest, cutting out a hollow with their dagger-pointed bills, much to the disgust and inconvenience of the legitimate tenants. But it would be useless trying to use that same nest again. It was not there.

The termites long since had plastered it over and removed all signs of bird occupancy.

Stocky, wedge-shaped Old Jack was in no hurry to begin work. There would be time enough for that when his mate became insistent, and forced him to get a move on. Old Jack did not know where she was at that precise moment. Half an hour previously she had left him and gone off on some business of her own. Jack didn't care. The sun was warm on his feathers and he felt at peace with everyone.

Giving a low, gurgling laugh to indicate his contentment, he fluffed out his feathers and settled down on the limb, his big beak on his breast, like an ungainly, lumpy feather-duster. But appearances are deceptive. Though his wings were broad and stiff and were hardly the type to sustain a bird on a long flight, they were designed by Nature to turn him into a death-dealing feathered bullet. With those wings of his he could dive like an arrow on his prey, with his sharp beak straight out like a lance. Though not as handsome as many of the bush birds, he was by no means drab. His olive-brown back was checked with lighter hues, while his wing feathers were blackish-brown, some tipped with metallic green. On his white breast he had a series of faint brown bars, while his tail was rich brown, banded with black and tipped with white.

Like most of his bush colleagues, Old Jack had a variety of nicknames. Officially called laughing kookaburra, he also answered to the titles of brown kingfisher, great kingfisher, giant kingfisher, bushman's clock, and settler's clock. Certain folk with a sense of humour had labelled him "Ha ha pigeon." The "ha ha" was certainly there, but any bird less like a pigeon in looks and habits it would be hard to find. As to Old Jack being a kingfisher, that was the greatest joke of all. Old Jack couldn't catch a fish if he tried, unless one happened to be trapped in a few inches of shallow water. The "fish" he was most adept at securing had feathers, not scales, for he was a great nest robber, stealing young birds and eating them as fast and as often as he was able.

Old Jack had a slightly over-rated reputation as a snake-killer. He killed them all right and ate them, too, but they were not very big ones. He would tackle them, but, after all, there was a limit to his strength.

It may have been the recollection of these matters that caused the kookaburra suddenly to burst forth into a full-throated gale of loud laughter. His cackling call, starting with a chuckle, rang through the gum trees, causing many small birds to pause in their daily round and gaze at each other in wild surmise before vanishing discreetly among the denser thickets. Not that they had much to worry about. Old Jack rarely attacked adult birds, no matter how small. They were too hard to catch. But their nestlings were another matter. And judging by the activity around him, the bush soon would be filled with nests which, in turn, would be filled with plump young chicks.

Perched on his limb, Old Jack took note of everything that was going on. He marked with interest the activities of a pair of grey butcherbirds who were constructing a cup-shaped nest of twigs, bits of roots, dead grass and other material in the upright forked branch of a blue gum a few hundred yards away. The birds seemed happy in their work, for now and again they gave their rich, mellow, flute-like call as they darted backwards and forwards collecting nest material. In due course, the female bird would lay her three or four eggs of pale greyish-green, blotched with reddishbrown.

Like Old Jack, the butcher-birds included nestling birds in their menu, but unlike the kookaburra, who confined himself to chicks, they thought nothing of lunching off the parent birds as well. Old Jack appreciated the butcher-birds' habit of keeping larders. They hung their victims on thorns or sharp twigs or in the forks of trees, to be eaten when they felt like it. As a dog buried a bone against a future snack, the butchers, if they caught a small bird or a lizard or some other morsel and they were not hungry, would impale it through the neck on the thorn or sharp twig. Old Jack appreciated it because he often secured a free meal by raiding a larder when the butchers were not looking.

The butcher-birds had a great advantage over the kookaburra, in that they were equipped with vicious hooked beaks which enabled them to secure and hold their prey. Old Jack's beak, though huge, sharp and powerful, was pointed and had to be used as a spear. Nevertheless, the kookaburra very rarely went hungry.

He had no further leisure to spy on his neighbours, for at that moment there was a flurry of wings and his mate landed at his side. In her huge bill was a skink lizard. Old Jack immediately made a grab for it, but she was too quick for him. She flew on to another limb where she wasted no time in swallowing the lizard. Then she gave a derisive cackle and flew away, Old Jack following. She did not stop until she reached a big stringy bark nearly a quarter of a mile away, and then she alighted on a branch very close to a big black globular out-cropping which resembled a gumboil on an aborigine's jaw.

Old Jack knew that it was a termites' nest, and he knew also that it was time for him to do a bit of hard work.

Inside the tree dwelt a colony of termites, or white ants, although they were neither white nor ants. They were of a dirty grey colour and there were literally millions of them, living in a complicated series of galleries, tunnels and chambers. Deep down in a special cell dwelt the colony queen, who was an enormous grub-like creature fully two inches long and capable of laying up to 5,000 eggs a day. As the eggs were laid, the armies of workers carried them away to various nurseries where they cared for them until they hatched.

The termites, all of them blind, were divided into two families, workers and soldiers. The soldiers had big jaws and heads, and their task was to protect the workers while they went about their jobs. The workers also had to feed these soldiers, who could not do so themselves because of the remarkable size and shape of their heads.

These termites were of the wood-dwelling variety and lived entirely inside the tree. They shunned the light; in fact, owing to their delicate bodies, sunlight was death to them. Should they wish to emerge to the outer exposed tree trunk, they first built a roof or overhead gallery of mud or chewed-up wood. It was in such out-croppings, some of them enormous, that Jack Kookaburra and his tribe built their nests after excavating a hole large enough to accommodate a family. It was hard work, but it had to be done.

Old Jack and his mate had two methods. Sometimes, in turn, they would cling to the outcropping and hammer at the hard crust with their dagger-sharp beaks like a human using a road drill; their second method was to fly a short distance, wheel around and charge the desired spot with beak outstretched, like a knight of old jousting in the lists with a lance, or a modern soldier taking part in a bayonet charge.

It was a task that, once commenced, had to be completed. Should the birds cease work for any length of time, their labours would go for naught, because the hordes of working termites, guarded by their soldiers, would quickly plug the hole. The soldiers were no trouble to Old Jack and his mate—they merely swept the grotesque insects out of the way. But if the birds took a whole day off, they could rest assured that when they returned to work, they would find that their time had been wasted. Once they were in occupancy and Mrs. Old Jack was incubating her eggs, the termites would give it up as a bad job and sidestep the outcropping.

With the job well under way, Old Jack and his mate decided to have a brief spell and knock off for lunch. As to what would form this snack, they had no decided preference. It was merely a question as to what was the nearest thing to eat and the easiest to obtain. Their nesting tree stood with others near a large waterhole, with a big outcropping of rocks nearby. This was good feeding territory, because frogs and yabbies were to be had at the waterhole—provided they were incautious enough to come out on the land, and the habit of lizards and other reptiles to bask in the sun on the rocks provided the kookaburras with enough potential for a repast.

Old Jack Kookaburra and his mate were not the only bush creatures who saw in the waterhole and its surroundings a fruitful source of meal tickets. There were certain others who enjoyed feeding off frogs, lizards, birds and the smaller animals, noteworthy among these being a family of tiger snakes who had lived in the area long before the kookaburras had found their termites' nest.

This snake family lurked in a disused rabbit burrow which had been dug under the pile of rocks, and consisted of a mother and fifteen young ones. The old snake was six feet long, sleek and well fed, as were her infants, who only measured inches where she stretched for feet. Like all her kind, she preferred swampy areas or any places where there was water, and she was quite an expert swimmer.

Coiled up in her burrow with her young ones around her, the old snake had no worries or troubles. She had fed well earlier in the day on sundry frogs she had managed to strike down as they squatted idly on stones and debris at the water's edge. If she had been without a family, she would have been outside basking in the sun on a hollow log, or even upon the rocks, but the instinct to protect her youngsters and not expose them to possible danger had caused her to forego that luxury. She had a six-foot-six mate somewhere, but she did not see much of him. He came and went as the mood took him.

The rabbit hole was eight or nine feet deep, but she was not at the extreme end; in fact she was no more than three feet from the entrance, which was partly covered by some dangling couch grass.

And as she lay there peacefully, with malice towards none, her head pointing towards the back of the burrow, she was rudely disturbed by the end of a stick which prodded her sharply in her coiled body.

Swinging her head swiftly around, she buffeted the stick, which disappeared. Alarmed and angry, she fell into the characteristic attitude of the tiger snake about to strike, with the front part of her body raised from the ground and the head and the skin on her neck flattened out. But there was nothing to strike at.

Tiger Snake was perturbed and restless. Something inimical to her welfare was outside her burrow and evidently intended to attack her. She was quite ready to defend herself and her family against anything on four legs, two legs or no legs, but she could not see what menaced her. Possessing a family, she did not feel inclined to desert them to investigate. It was better to be cautious and alert and allow the menace to reveal itself.

So she maintained her striking attitude and waited. She did not have long. Her wicked eyes, glaring at the burrow entrance, saw something coming towards her. It looked like another snake, except that it was in midair and not crawling along the ground. She soon recognised it as a long stick, and she was not afraid of sticks, even this one which seemed to have developed wings. It was a danger, however, and she hissed and lunged. Her head hit the stick with all the power of her strong, tensed body, and again it vanished.

Outside the burrow, Scotty Macdonald turned to Egghead and Tiger Birch and waved the stick in the air.

"There's something down there all right, but whether it is a rabbit or not, I'm hanged if I know," he confessed. "I've poked the stick in twice and each time something has bashed it hard."

"It couldn't be a rabbit," said young Birch. "A rabbit wouldn't bash a stick, and anyway, I'll bet a thousand quid that there are no rabbits around here. There might have been once, but not now. If there were any in that hole, you would see signs of them."

"Maybe it's a wombat," suggested Scotty.

"It would be a pretty small wombat to get into that hole," said Tiger, shaking his head. "Wombats are as big as pigs."

"Maybe it is a big snake," said Egghead. "Could easily be," said Scotty. "Snakes dig holes and live in them."

"They don't," said Tiger. "No snake of any kind digs a hole. If you ever find a snake in a hole, something else dug it. Snakes just can't dig holes. They generally go for hollow logs, or even camp under bits of bark, but they take over holes in the ground, too."

"If you like, I'll put my arm down the hole and feel around," offered Egghead.

"Don't be so silly," said Tiger. "If there is a snake down there you'd get bitten. Here, give me that waddy and let me have a poke. And stand clear in case something comes out of it."

He took the stick from Scotty and plunged it into the hole, waggling it about furiously. He felt something trembling and again rotated the stick vigorously.

This was something more than snake flesh and blood could stand. The old tiger snake, enraged by the rough end of the stick scraping over her body and tickling her numerous ribs, hurled herself on to it, crushing it to the ground and wrenching it out of young Birch's hand.

"Stand clear," he yelled, "there is something down that hole and it might dive out and grab one of us. Stand clear, both of you!"

As Scotty and Egghead leaped back, eyeing the hole warily, Scotty asked anxiously, "What are we going to do, Tiger? I think we'd better leave things alone."

"Make a fire and smoke the thing out, no matter what it is," said Tiger.

"Listen, Tiger, I don't like messing around with snakes." Scotty's voice was uneasy. "I say we shoot through and leave it alone. Anyway, you're always the bloke who tells everyone to leave the bush things alone."

"It might not be a snake. If it is, it ought to be killed. If it isn't, a bit of smoke won't hurt it," rejoined Tiger. "I always like to see what is going on and learn what I can about the bush; therefore I'm going to smoke out whatever is down that hole. Help me gather some wood."

"That's a waste of time unless you've found some matches since we left the creek," said Egghead.

"Remember, we couldn't make a fire to dry Humpy Campbell's clothes."

"H'm, you're right," grunted Tiger. "Here, let's have another go with that stick. But keep well out of the way, you jokers."

Tiger picked up the stick again and jabbed it viciously

into the burrow. This time he succeeded in pinning one of the infant snakes to the ground, causing it to wriggle in distress. This was the last straw for the old mother snake. Tiger withdrew the stick and prepared for another jab, but he did not make it; for, following the stick as it withdrew from the hole, came something that made the boy shudder in fright. It was the deadliest thing in the Australian bush, an angry tiger snake coming at a fast wriggle and bent on revenge.

"Get for your lives," he yelled in terror. Scotty and Egghead, who had been standing well back, were momentarily frozen stiff by the rapid turn of events, and just stared at the oncoming snake as if petrified. The angry reptile reared up to strike at the terrified boys who cowered only a few feet from it, and was on the point of launching its wicked head at Scotty, when there came a great flurry of wings and the reptile was knocked sideways by a huge pointed beak.

Old Jack Kookaburra up in his gum tree with his mate had witnessed the whole of the proceedings. He had wondered what the three boys were up to, but as they had not interfered in his affairs, he had stayed put. But a snake was something that he understood very well.

The kookaburra struck the tiger snake behind the neck and still had hold of it as its head hit the ground. Scotty and Egghead unfroze and ran to join Tiger, who stood at a safe distance watching, awe-stricken, the strange combat.

A deep-seated instinct had caused Old Jack to grab the snake by the neck and thus keep away from its deadly fangs. The bird, however, had caught a Tartar. The old snake was not going calmly to allow him to make an end of her. Six feet of her elongated body began to thresh wildly about, and once she almost succeeded in wrapping a coil around the big bird. Had Old Jack been a wedge-tailed eagle, or one of the larger hawks, he could have seized the snake's body in two very powerful talons and thus had three grips instead of one. As it was, he could use only his beak. That fact, and the weight of the fully-grown snake, were against ultimate success.

With wings flapping strongly, the kookaburra attempted to lift the snake bodily from the ground. He got her up a few feet, but she dragged him down again by sheer weight and energetic writhing.

Out of the tree above him echoed a loud burst of harsh laughter. Mrs. Kookaburra was taking a keen interest in the matter.

"Come down and help him instead of laughing, you fool!" roared Tiger Birch.

And, just as if she had understood what the boy had said, Mrs. Kookaburra launched herself from the bough and shot downwards, to land near the struggling combatants.

Too fascinated to interfere even if they had been game to, the three watching boys saw the female kookaburra dodging the snake's lashing tail. Then, as the reptile straightened out for a moment, she seized her chance and grabbed its tail about a foot from the tip. Flapping her wings powerfully, she rose slowly into the air. Old Jack, his beak still gripping the snake just behind its head, rose too, and between them they managed to lift the writhing reptile well clear of the ground.

It was an amazing sight for the three boys. The powerful snake wriggled madly, waving the tenacious birds about in the air as if they were feathered flags, while they hung on grimly. Slowly they rose until they were about twelve feet up, and then an extra convulsive wriggle on the part of the snake caused Old Jack to let go his hold. The snake dropped swiftly, and Mrs. Kookaburra on the other end was pulled downwards a few feet before she could release her grip. The snake hit the ground with its head right at the entrance of the burrow and before the kookaburras could seize her again, she had vanished into safety.

The two birds stood near the burrow entrance, but did not attempt to enter; and as they stood there, mourning one lost meal, they were provided with another. Three of the infant tiger snakes, each about six inches long, came wriggling out of the hole. Quick as a flash, each bird seized one in its beak, bashed it several times against the rocks, threw back a feathered head and calmly swallowed its catch. The third young snake headed towards the waterhole, but Old Jack was on it before it got any distance. It, too, went the way of its brothers.

Then, rising lazily into the air, both birds flew back to the tree to resume their nest excavating.

"Well, and what do you know about that!" breathed Tiger Birch, mopping his brow with a filthy handkerchief. "I've often heard about it, and now I've actually seen it-kookaburras killing snakes!"

"They didn't kill the big one," Egghead observed.

"They would have if it hadn't escaped back into its hole," said Scotty. "They would have kept at it until they did. One of them couldn't have killed it on his own, but the two of them together would have fixed its clock for it."

"I dunno," said Tiger thoughtfully. "It was a whopper and I doubt if they could have carried it up high enough to keep dropping it. Anyway, they know where it is and it will have to be on guard every day. And if there are any more young ones in the hole, those two kookaburras will clean them all up in time."

"They saved our lives," said Egghead solemnly. "We would have been bitten to death by that snake if they had not come to our aid."

"One of us would have, anyway," said Scotty. "And that would have been me as I was the closest. Thanks, Jack," he yelled at the busy kookaburras up at the termites' nest.

"Sweet pretty creature," came a voice from the top of the rock out-crop.

"Hey, by heck, that little joker gets around, doesn't he?" ejaculated Tiger Birch. "That is, if he is the same bird we saw down near the creek a few hours ago when Humpy made a goat of himself."

"The bush is crammed with wagtails," said Scotty. "It couldn't be the same."

But it was. The banksias into which Willy had fled from Humpy Campbell were not very far away from the waterhole and Willy had been catching insects around it when the boys arrived. He had witnessed everything that had occurred, but, for once in his inquisitive life, had not attempted to interfere between kookaburra and snake.

They were three very subdued boys who continued their walk in the bush. As for Old Jack and his mate, excavating their nest in the termite mound, it had been all in the day's work. As for Willy Wagtail... well, that applied to him also!

CHAPTER FIVE
BUSH JUSTICE

THESE were very busy days for Willy Wagtail and his mate. Their three eggs had hatched and most of their time was now occupied in feeding their hungry chicks.

Mrs. Willy kept to the nest a great deal during the first week of the nestlings' lives. The unclad youngsters had a warm and well-lined nest, but it was open to the skies, and Mrs. Willy had to spend much of her time sitting on it and maintaining the young naked bodies at an even temperature. This meant that Willy had to keep five mouths, including his own, going. Of course, his mate did leave the nest from time to time to do her share of the feeding. But the little chicks were growing and feathering fast, and soon would fill the nest. Mrs. Willy then would not have to brood over them at all.

As long as daylight lasted, Willy was foraging for food. At night he stood guard, and very little sleep he got. There were many night raiders only too ready to deprive him of his family. Owls on moth-like wings, stealthy tiger and native cats, crawling tree snakes and other deadly creatures had to be guarded against. Not that there was any greater safety under sunny skies. Hawks, butcherbirds, kookaburras, sneaking lizards and goannas and even an odd magpie were all menaces. Actually it was not safe to leave the nest unguarded for one moment, but it had to be done if the family were to be fed.

At times during the long night hours, Willy, perched near his nest and getting what sleep he could, became as talkative as he did during the day. His "sweet pretty creature" and "did-ja-didja-did" rang out at intervals, a warning to everyone that he was on sentry duty and intruders did so at their own risk.

For a little bird as inquisitive as Willy Wagtail, domestic duties were quite a burden. There was a great deal going on in the bush and around the creek for him to inspect and superintend, and he could not spare the time. He was like a small boy forced to stay at home and be nice to some old battle-axe of an aunt when his favourite cowboy film was on at the local picture theatre.

But wagtail nature being what it was, Willy had his off-moments. He was not always the perfect devotee to domestic duty.

On his way back to the willow tree one morning, Willy was passing the group of banksias when he heard a mild uproar of bird voices. He slowed down a little, made a half-swerve towards the trees, remembered his errand and darted a few more yards in the direction of the willow trees, and then, as the uproar grew louder, he swerved around and headed for the banksias, coming to rest on a twig on the nearest tree. In his beak he held a small grasshopper, intended for his youngsters.

The banksia adjacent to the one in which he perched was the scene of the disturbance. Willy saw four birds and they seemed to be at variance and discontented with one another. Willy identified them as a pair of blue-faced honeyeaters and a couple of white-browed babblers. On the branch on which the four birds were wrangling was a dome-shaped nest with a side entrance. It was lined with grass and bits of wool and hair and had been built by the babblers. The discussion was about which pair of birds was going to use it.

There was nothing to prevent the honeyeaters from building their own nest of sticks and twigs with a cupped centre lined with strips of bark, grass and horsehair. They had done it before, but only when there had been no babblers' homes to steal. For the whole tribe of blue-faced honeyeaters were great thieves. They preferred the nests of babblers, but they were not above taking those of noisy miners or soldier birds, wattle birds, or even magpies; but, being great tacticians as well as great thieves, they never tried to take a magpie's nest when Maggie was in actual possession. They waited until Maggie had done with his nest and had no further use for it before moving in, relining it and raising their own thieving brood.

Some of these honeyeaters had been known to steal a babbler's nest apparently from sheer force of habit. Having dispossessed the rightful owners, they built their own unattractive nest on top of the babbler's, flattening it to size and shape.

The babblers in the banksia had almost completed their nest and, not unnaturally, wanted it for themselves. The honeyeaters were just as determined to steal it and, being more pugnacious than the babblers, had that advantage over them.

And so there was a great to-do in the banksia tree. Amid much fluttering of wings, chattering, chirping and beak-snapping, the dispute went on with Willy Wagtail acting as self-appointed referee. He could not add his voice to the din because his beak was filled with grasshopper, but he sat on his twig, his huge tail swaying with excitement, and looked on. But when one of the babblers hopped into the nest and, with head poking out of the side door defied the honeyeaters to eject it, Willy swallowed the small grasshopper and then darted across and perched on the same limb as the squabbling quartet.

The babbler in the nest babbled at the honeyeaters while its mate stood on the limb with snapping beak and wings lifted menacingly. The unperturbed honeyeaters were not the least intimidated by this. It was not the first nest they had stolen and they were used to this display of resistance from babblers. They both lunged together and the babbler on the limb was knocked off it.

"Sweet pretty creature!" shouted Willy, but whether he was barracking the babblers or the honeyeaters was not clear. The blue-faces inspected him briefly, dismissed him as of no account, and while one kept an eye on the babbler who had been knocked off the limb, the other dived into the nest. There was a convulsive heaving and the babbler inside shot out, leaving the triumphant honeyeater in possession. That finished it. The flustered babblers flew away, chirping disconsolately, to make another home in a distant place.

Willy hopped close to the stolen nest and was rewarded with a peck from one of the honeyeaters. His dignity hurt, he chattered sharply and swung back to another limb in another banksia. This limb was near the top of the tree and sitting on it was another bird who had been a very silent spectator of the nest theft.

She was a very handsome female bronze cuckoo who had not been in the district very long. Unlike Willy Wagtail and the peewits, who lived around the creek and the farms all the year through, the cuckoo and her mate spent their winters in the far north. They had departed towards the end of the previous summer, and had returned, now that spring had come, to breed.

Cuckoo was hated by all the small birds in the area in which she decided to settle. She did not, of course, build her own nest. She selected one made by any of the numerous small birds who laid eggs of a somewhat similar colour.

It was the first cuckoo Willy had seen that season and he did not like it a bit. He announced the fact by chattering loudly and making a deliberate attack on the cuckoo. The honeyeaters heard his call and knew what it meant. Together they left their stolen nest and joined Willy in harassing the unwelcome intruder. Birds might have differences amongst themselves, but they combined against cuckoos.

The newcomer had been perched silently on the high branch of the banksia before Willy had first come upon the scene. She had been very interested in the babblers' nest, and had been quietly prospecting the whole layout. As soon as she and her mate had arrived in the district a week earlier, they both had quietly scouted around for a suitable home for their future family. They required one with a side entrance. A fairy wren's, a thornbill's, a warbler's, a babbler's—any one of these would do as long as the owners were insect-eaters. There were dozens of different types from which to choose. One season she had made the mistake of placing her egg in the nest of a diamond sparrow or spottedsided finch, and the youngster, when hatched, had died of starvation because the finches, naturally, had fed it with seeds,

Having noted the nest-building of the babblers, the cuckoos had decided that it was just what they needed. All that remained for them to do was to keep a close check on its progress and, at the right time, slip their egg into it. It needed the exercise of the keenest judgment, but that was second nature to the cuckoos. The age-old plan was to wait until the foster-birds had completed their nest and had laid their eggs, and then, at the opportune time, touring the changes." This was done by the female cuckoo laying her egg on the ground, picking it up in her beak, flying up and slipping it into the selected nest and removing one of the other eggs therefrom so that the clutch would be complete.

Deep-seated instinct told the cuckoo that if she laid her egg before the foster-parents commenced to brood, they would either throw hers out or desert the nest altogether. Again, if she laid it after the foster-mother had commenced to incubate her own clutch, it might not be hatched at all.

Having decided on the babblers' nest, the cuckoos waited patiently until the time was ripe. The female kept a close and unobtrusive watch upon it, unseen by the builders. When the honeyeaters had come along and dispossessed the babblers, it had meant no change in her plan. They would do equally as well for foster-parents.

It had been left to Bush Busybody No. 1 to upset her calculations. Willy Wagtail had seen her and, unable to keep his big beak shut, had had to go and tell the whole country-side of her presence. It might mean that she would have to completely revise her whole planning. Time would show.

The honeyeaters were not going to have a cuckoo hanging around the place and they demonstrated that fact by the vicious attack they made on her. Willy Wagtail was up to his black-and-white neck in it, of course. He was not alone. Most of the small birds in the vicinity joined in the fray. Noisy miners, thornbills, little fairy wrens, a couple of Jack Winters and a passing yellow robin took to that cuckoo. And, strange to relate, the cuckoo actually welcomed the attack. It could have made things unpleasant for one or two of the smaller birds, but that was not its design. It flew rapidly away, followed by the whole flock of birds, Willy Wagtail in the lead and the honeyeaters not far behind. They gave up the chase when the cuckoo had, in their opinion, been driven far enough away from the banksias. Then they all dispersed, each to his or her own business. Last to leave, of course, was Willy Wagtail. He used language to the fleeing cuckoo which was quite unnecessary before wheeling away to collect fresh food for his nestlings in the willow.

Bronze cuckoo was quite satisfied with her morning's work. It had been a perfect rehearsal for the actual performance within a week's time. All she had to do was to wait. The honeyeaters might make one or two structural alterations to the babblers' stolen nest, but within the week, at the outside, their four or five salmon-coloured, purplish-red blotched eggs would have been laid. The cuckoo's own egg would be olive-green coloured, but in the darkness of the domed nest's interior, the difference would never be noticed by the honeyeaters.

And, so bronze cuckoo composed herself to wait, staying as close as possible to the nesting tree without being observed. She was not so much concerned about the honeyeaters as about that bush gossip and tale-bearer, Willy Wagtail. If anyone was likely to give the game away it would be him.

At last the day arrived when she judged it expedient to act. Early in the morning, just before sunrise, she took up her position in a banksia unseen by the honeyeaters and Willy Wagtail. That little villain was at home in his willow, and the honeyeaters were roosting in their own tree, with the female in the nest and the male on a nearby twig. The female cuckoo was hidden from their sight. The next move was up to her mate. His was the job to lure the honeyeaters away, and when she was ready it would not matter if Willy Wagtail and all his friends and relations were present.

Just as the sun came up, the male cuckoo made his appearance as scheduled. He flew close to the banksias and perched on an old stump in full view. He wanted to be seen. His mournful song, "pee-e, pee-e, pee-e," drifted through the trees and brought the male honeyeater to instant alert. It gave a loud call, which brought its mate's head popping out of the nest. There was no need for discussion. Both birds dashed at the cuckoo, which instantly took flight, heading towards the creek, travelling just fast enough for the honeyeaters to keep up with it. Its strategy was to lure them away while its mate put the master-plan into operation.

No sooner were the honeyeaters out of the way, than she dropped to the earth, laid her egg, seized it gently in her beak, and flew up to the nest. Clinging to the side, she deftly popped the egg into the chamber among the four already there. Quickly taking up a honeyeater's egg in her bill, she fled away, dropping it in flight. Five minutes later, the honeyeaters, having hounded the male cuckoo, as they fondly thought, to a safe distance, returned to the nest. A brief examination showed everything in order. The hen bird quickly popped into the nest and crouched on the four eggs.

After that, life flowed along peacefully. Nothing more was seen of the cuckoos, and the honeyeater sat patiently on the eggs until they were hatched. One afternoon she felt a faint stirring under her. The first nestling had appeared. Carefully she removed the two halves of broken shell and awaited the arrival of the rest of the family. Two more eggs hatched that night and the fourth just before daybreak next morning.

One of the nestlings was quite unlike his three fellow-lodgers. He was bigger and of a different colour. All four were completely naked and totally blind and as they moved feebly in the nest, there was no hint of the tragedy to come—a tragedy enacted thousands of times in the bush over the years; a tragedy that would be enacted as long as there were cuckoos and other birds to rear their young ones for them.

That afternoon the young cuckoo began to get restless. The slightest movements of his nest companions seemed to irritate him beyond measure. Squirming and twisting, he arched his back until he succeeded in jamming one of the young honeyeaters against the side of the nest. Then, with a backward push, he managed to work it towards the entrance and literally heave it out. The small bird fell to the ground.

There was peace in the nest for only a few moments and then a second honeyeater chick chanced to fall across the little cuckoo's back. A convulsive shudder shook his frame and, with a backing motion, he got to the entrance and threw the smaller bird out. The third and last followed within a couple of minutes, leaving the baby cuckoo in sole and undisputed occupancy.

Thus Mother Nature's law that the strong shall survive and the weaker shall perish had been carried out once more. There would not have been enough room in that nest for any birds other than the cuckoo as he grew rapidly. There would not have been enough food for all. Therefore, the other occupants had to die that he might survive. Among the many secrets jealously guarded by Mother Nature was how a new-born, sightless, infant, naked bird had the instinct and sense of direction to find the entrance of a nest and from it cast into death the small rivals which, had they been permitted to survive, would have menaced its own existence.

The cynical Gods of Bush Tragedy, however, had not yet completed their grim jest in that grove of banksias.

Some days after the infant honeyeaters had been ejected from their home to provide meals for a swarm of ants which had a mound nearby, Old Jack Kookaburra, roaming around the countryside in search of food for his own lusty tribe of youngsters now squawking in the excavated termites' nest, arrived at the grove. He swooped down for a short rest and had hardly landed before he spotted the honeyeaters' nest. Both birds were absent, frantically trying to collect enough food to satisfy the enormous appetite of their equally enormous foster-child, whose head projected from the nest entrance while its owner squawked hungrily.

Old Jack eyed the nest and the head of the young cuckoo and gave a gurgle of satisfaction. Sidling along the limb, he shot out his wicked beak and literally tore the youngster from its hiding place. With a quick flick of the head, he bashed the huge chick against the limb and then took off, heading straight for the termites' nest.

Thus was forged the last link in a chain of bush justice. The babblers' nest had been stolen by the honeyeaters; the honeyeaters' youngsters had been murdered by a young cuckoo; and Old Jack Kookaburra had murdered the murderer.

Equally tragic, perhaps, was the melancholy fact that Willy Wagtail, the bush newspaper, had missed all but the very first episode of the story.

Small wonder that Old Jack laughed and laughed as he fed his youngsters in the depths of his termite nest.

CHAPTER SIX

SWAMP ADVENTURE

AWAY across the rich farming lands, and forming a distant boundary of the Campbell property, the swamplands covered a large area. It was the chosen hunting, feeding and nesting place of numerous wild birds. Around its edges dignified ibis, graceful spoonbills, hoarse-croaking herons, egrets, blue cranes and other birds sought their food and built their nests in secluded places among the reeds and rushes. On the surface of the water swam waterhens, wild duck and other waterfowl, while, in the skies above, hawks, harriers and kestrels kept watch and ward, ever ready to take toll of any small birds incautious enough to show themselves.

Humpy Campbell's father owned a large, flat-bottomed punt in which he often cruised among the reeds and tall swamp grasses with his rifle, for the hunting was good. Black duck, waterhen, plover and snipe were plentiful and often formed part of the menu in the Campbell home.

Mr. Campbell, in particular, liked snipe, but these birds were timid and wary, and not easy to shoot. Though known as "Australian snipe" and, by Jimmy and his mates, "Jack Snipe," this handsome, long-billed, speckled bird was a cosmopolitan globe-trotter, as much at home, if not more, in Japan. In fact, Jack Snipe used the Land of the Rising Sun as his breeding ground, his mate laying her stone-coloured, blotched eggs in a depression in the ground along the shores of some Japanese marsh. The birds spent from May to July in Japan, and then took the long journey southwards, arriving in flocks in Australia in August or September. Here they spent the hot summer days in the swamplands and along the river flats and marshes, departing north again in March or April, before winter set in.

Plover, too, was a very shy bird, needing much patience to stalk. Spurwing haunted the edges of the swamp and was very popular with all the other birds owing to his habit of informing the world when danger was apparent. Mr. Campbell often had reason to say rude things when some bird he was stalking took fright and vanished on hearing the spurwing plover's shrill call of alarm. His loud "kurra-carrack, kurra-carrack" alerted every living creature within a wide radius.

Humpy Campbell had been told on numerous occasions that he was never to take the punt out on the swamp without an adult being with him. Under the bright rays of the sun, the swamp was an ever-changing composition of light and shadow as the breeze played with the reed tops and grasses, but it was also a treacherous area of deep holes, submerged logs and clinging mud in which a boy might become stuck fast, far from shore, without hope of rescue should he be trapped alone.

As Humpy poled the punt through the reeds he never gave a thought to these matters. It was Saturday afternoon, and his parents were in town at the picture theatre. The punt was roomy, but there was little space to spare when Scotty, Tiger and Egghead were in it with him. Tiger sat up in the front, with Egghead and Scotty in the middle, while

Humpy stood at the back and used the punt pole like a veteran. The lad was an expert, because he had had plenty, if illicit, practice in the art.

The boys had taken the punt with no other idea than to have a cruise around the swamp, and perhaps find some targets for their catapults. So far the hunting had been fruitless, as the noise they made, singing and shouting, had effectually placed all the swamp inhabitants on guard.

One pair of birds who did not take much notice of the boys was a couple of cormorants, or black shags, perched on two old fence-posts sticking up out of the water. They were fishing and refused to be disturbed. Every now and then, one of the shags would dive from its post after a fish and then return to the perch to eat its catch. Sometimes the birds dived in and stayed submerged, chasing their prey under water. They were accomplished swimmers and therefore never went without a meal.

"Look at that flight of birds up there," remarked Egghead. "Would they be ducks, do you think?"

Humpy squinted heavenwards and located the flight. There were between thirty and forty birds, travelling in V-formation, one line of the V being longer than the other.

"They're a bit far away to tell, Egghead," he said, "but I'd guess they were ibis. There are lots of them on the swamps these days."

"I fancy they're pelicans," said Scotty. "What do you say, Tiger?" Tiger Birch screwed up his eyes and took a long look before pronouncing judgment.

"Black swans," he said briefly.

"Ibis," said Humpy.

"Pelicans," said Scotty.

"How can you be sure that they are swans, Tiger?" asked Egghead. "Might they not be pelicans?"

"Definitely not pelicans," said Tiger. "Have you ever seen pelicans flying in that formation? Pelicans fly in a single line, side by side, not in a V. Ibis fly in a V with one arm longer than the other, and so do swans; but swans are always changing formation, each bird taking the lead as the other gets tired. If you watch them long enough, you'll notice that the V keeps changing its size. As the leader drops back, and another bird takes over, one arm gets longer and longer and the other, of course, shorter and shorter, until at length they are flying in a line, but not one behind the other. The line is a slanting one. Then the leading bird will drop back again and the next one takes first place; then so on and so on until the V is formed once more. This only happens on very long flights, of course. Ibis fly much the same."

"But why don't they just fly one behind the other in a straight line?" Egghead wanted to know.

"They couldn't," replied Tiger. "The leading bird creates a slipstream like an aeroplane and it would interfere with the flying of any bird straight behind. No, all these birds always fly about a wingspan to the right or the left of each other."

Even though Scotty and Humpy felt disposed to argue the point with Tiger, they were only halfhearted about it. They recognised, rightly, that with all his reading and his thirst for first-hand knowledge in the bush, he always knew what he was talking about as regards the habits of birds and animals.

As Humpy poled the punt along, he kept a sharp lookout for a likely place in which to anchor for a rest. He would not allow any of the other three to handle the punt pole. Presently he saw the top of an ancient stump sticking out of the reeds and he skilfully guided the craft towards it.

"We'll tie her up here, boys, while we have afternoon

tea," he announced. None of the others objected. It would not have mattered a scrap to Humpy if they had done so. He threw a rope around the stump and secured it to a ring in the punt's stern.

Afternoon tea consisted of the food that each of the lads had stolen from their home larders before departing on the excursion. Had any of them asked their mothers for something to eat, they probably would have got it, but that was not their way. Something secured easily was not half as precious as something taken without permission.

The pooled foodstuffs would scarcely have found favour at a Royal banquet. Humpy had brought along two shelled boiled eggs which he had found in the refrigerator. They had been prepared by his mother as part of a salad for the evening meal. He had wrapped them in a dirty handkerchief, and they looked like it.

Scotty Macdonald produced a piece of cake in which a marble and a dead match were embedded. He had not troubled to wrap it up, but had simply shoved it into his pocket. Tiger Birch had a dozen broken-up biscuits, while Egghead came to light with an unattractive-looking lump of material which he stated was a type of Continental liver sausage which his mother personally had constructed out of this and that. His friends eyed it doubtfully.

"Why can't you New Australians eat decent tucker?" demanded Humpy, who was not celebrated for his courtesy and good manners. "That looks like nothing on earth."

"And probably tastes like it," put in Scotty.

"It tastes good," defended Egghead. "You try a bit."

"Okay," replied Scotty. "I'll eat anything that's eatable."

"Me too," said Humpy—a fact that his friends knew. Humpy had been known to dip cake in vinegar and down it with apparent relish. They were munching their motley feed when Egghead remarked:—

"That is a funny-looking bird over there. It looks like a duck with a snake for its neck and head." He pointed to a patch of clear water a hundred yards away.

"Some people call it the snake bird," said Tiger Birch. "It is a darter. Get an eyeful of its neck with the kink in it. And see that long beak it's got. It swims under water and spears fish with that beak. The kink in its neck acts like a spring. It can shoot its neck out like an arrow."

"Watch me make it move," said Humpy, fitting a stone in the pouch of his catapult and letting fly. His shot was wide, but as it hit the water and skipped along the surface, the darter took fright and dived. Then, with its body quite submerged and only its neck and head above water, it swam rapidly away.

"That does look funny," laughed Egghead. "You would think it was a snake swimming along."

"I bet you wished that tiger snake had swum away when you poked at it in the rabbit burrow that day," chuckled Humpy. "Gosh, I wish I had been there. I would have killed the thing on the spot."

"We know that," said Tiger. "You can't expect Egghead and Scotty and me to have enough courage for that. We're just a pack of dingoes."

"No need to be sarcastic," snorted Humpy. "At least I wouldn't have been silly enough to go poking sticks down its hole."

"How did we know there was a snake in the hole?" hooted Tiger. "Anyway, I'm sick and tired of having you throw it up at us, Humpy. A man is a fool to tell you anything. You always sling off."

"Yes, Humpy, quit it, or we'll chuck you out of the punt," grunted Scotty.

"You and who else?" said Humpy truculently. "Anyway, forget about the dashed snake. We don't want any brawls in this punt."

There was silence for a moment or two and then Humpy, idly glancing around the swamp, his catapult still in his hand, sighted two reed warblers. They were both clinging to the stem of a rush and one was feeding the other. A mother bird and her chick. The baby was fluttering its wings and had its beak open wide to receive the tasty morsel from its parent. Stealthily Humpy took aim with his catapult.

"Don't shoot those birds, Humpy!" exclaimed Tiger. "Have a heart!"

Humpy fired. The stone whizzed straight to the mark and the mother warbler dropped lifelessly on to the surface of the water. The startled baby fled into the thick reeds.

"What made you do that, Humpy, you cruel coot?" demanded Tiger angrily. "Stone the crows, that was plain murder!"

"A terrible thing to do, Humpy," said Egghead sadly. "That is what the German Gestapo used to do in the war."

"I didn't think I'd hit it," mumbled Humpy. "Anyway, it was only a dashed warbler."

"Feeding a young one," exclaimed Tiger. "Now what do you think is going to happen to the baby bird, hey?"

"Its old man will feed it," mumbled Humpy, ashamed and sorry for his impulsive action, but not prepared to admit it openly.

"What can you expect from a Campbell?" said Scotty nastily. "They've always been killers, murderers and stand-over men since the year dot."

"Is that so?" retorted Humpy. "Yes, it is so. Remember Glencoe!" replied Scotty, pointing an accusing finger at Humpy. "You Campbells should never forget Glencoe."

"Never heard of the mug," grunted Humpy. "I don't know every one of your low mates, Scotty."

"Glencoe is a place, not a bloke, you ignorant coot!" said Scotty. "And don't crack so dumb. You know all about Glencoe."

"Yep," put in Tiger Birch. "It's a pretty little town in New South Wales about 80 miles from the Queensland border. I've been there. Cold as charity in the winter."

"Not that Glencoe, you ratbag," snorted Scotty. "This one is in Scotland, right up in the Highlands. It's where the Campbell mob sneaked up on the Macdonald clan when they weren't looking and murdered hundreds of them in their beds. So what chance had a mother reed warbler got?"

"When did all this happen?" asked Humpy, beginning to show some interest. "Perhaps my grandfather was there."

"It happened a couple of hundred years ago, but us Macdonalds have got long memories, Humpy. No wonder you Campbells don't like being reminded of it."

"Look, I don't know what the heck you are gassing about, Scotty," said Humpy peevishly. "Why did all us Campbells clean up all you Macdonalds? I bet your mob had been up to no good."

"You Campbells should talk! However, seeing that you don't seem to know the history of your own tough clique, I'll give you a lesson. There is nothing to be proud of."

"Listen, Scotty, get this into your thick head. I'm an Australian!" exclaimed Humpy. "So is my old man. It was my grandfather who came from Scotland, if you want to make anything out of it."

"The Scotch ain't any great shakes, anyhow," put in Tiger Birch. "Being Scotch didn't help G. A. Custer."

"Hey? What the heck are you gassing about, Tiger?" demanded Scotty. "Who is G. A. Custer? Who dragged him into this argument?"

"Gosh, you must have read about him!" exclaimed Tiger in astonishment. "Why, they made a picture out of his life. Errol Flynn was in it. He was the American general who got cleaned up by the Indians. Millions of them did him in."

"Oh, I've heard of him," said Scotty. "Yes, the Sioux Indians massacred him." Scotty pronounced the tribal name "Sy-ox."

"Soo," corrected Tiger.

"What do you mean, Soo?" asked Scotty, a little puzzled.

"That's the name of the Indian tribe. Sioux, pronounced Soo, not Sy-ox," explained Tiger.

"Is that Soo?" inquired Scotty, trying to be funny. "Anyway, what has Custer to do with Scotland? He was a Yank and by all accounts the greatest false-alarm of a general who ever rode a nag. Didn't he let a bunch of Sy-ox sneak up on him and finish him?"

"Listen, who's telling this yarn, you or me?" asked Tiger in annoyance. "You stick to the mob who wear kilts. I've read all about Custer. He was commander of the U.S. Seventh Cavalry and he got trapped by the Sioux at a river called the Little Big Horn away back in 1876. The Sioux massacred him and all his 600 men. Nice going, huh?"

"I'll say Soo," said Scotty, reluctant to forget that quip.

"Nice going for the redskins," said Humpy. "But what a silly name to call a river," said Egghead.

"I'm hanged if I know where Tiger got the nutty notion that General Custer was a Scot. He wasn't," said Scotty.

"In the book I read," explained Tiger, "it said that the marching song of the U.S. Seventh Cavalry was Garyowen and that's a Scotch song, isn't it?"

"Yes, but that doesn't make Custer wear kilts," said Humpy.

"Kilts!" howled young Macdonald. "Kilts! But what can you expect from a reed warbler-killing Campbell, as I said before? It's not kilts. It's the kilt. Scots wear the kilt, not kilts."

"Hanged if I can see any difference," shrugged Humpy. "Not that I'm likely to wear a skirt like a girl, or like you, Scotty. I've seen you parading around in a skirt with a whitewash brush hanging in front of you."

"That's a sporran!" Scotty's irate voice rose to a scream. "I'll throttle you yet, you Campbell coot."

"Aw, forget it and tell me the rest of the yarn about this shindig up at Ben Nevis, or Glen Lomond, or wherever it was."

"Glencoe!" bellowed Scotty. "No wonder you Campbells want to forget the place. And forget reed warblers too."

"Oh, for the love of Mike, will you get on with the yarn?" said Humpy wearily. "And just cut out these insults about the Campbells, will you? I've just about had enough of it, see? You're going the right way, Scotty, to stop a bunch of fives in the eye."

"Yeah? You won't be able to get another fifty Campbells in a hurry," sneered Scotty. "It would take that many to clean up one Macdonald."

"Hey, no brawling in the punt," said Tiger in alarm. "We'll all go overboard. There is no room here for fights."

"I'm not scared of this Scotch joker, punt or no punt. Come to that, I'll take the three of you on," offered Humpy belligerently. "However, I'll wait until we get to the shore. In the meantime I wish Scotty would finish this yarn about us handful of Campbells, greatly outnumbered, no doubt, squashing a whole clan of Macdonald squibs at this Glencoe joint."

"Up near the Queensland border," nodded Tiger. "Up in

the Scots Highlands! Listen, if there are any more of these interruptions, I'll throw the lot of you into the swamp."

"Oh, do get on with it, Scotty," instructed Humpy wearily. "I wouldn't be surprised if the old Campbell clan didn't kill off the Macdonalds because they talked too much."

"What can you expect..." began Scotty.

"From a Campbell," finished Humpy. "Well, I'll tell you—a lift under the ear if you don't finish the story."

"All right then. Give me a fair go. It was this way: when King James II was tossed off the English throne, they got William III over from Orange for the job. Then..."

"When did this happen?" interrupted Tiger.

"Oh, about 1689. Why?"

"Well, that's a dashed lie to start with," protested Tiger. "Orange is a town in New South Wales about fifty miles from Bathurst, and Australia wasn't discovered until donkey's years after 1689. So how could they possibly get a king from Orange, unless he was an aboriginal?"

"You paper-skulled rat bag!" shouted Scotty. "This Orange was in Holland. Now, shut up, will you! This William III became King of England. One of his best pals was a bird named Archie Campbell, who was first Duke of Argyll. This Campbell..."

"Argyll is a bit of a town about two miles from Goulburn in New South Wales, but they spell it Argyle for some reason," Tiger mentioned.

"This Campbell of Argyll," said Scotty, paying no attention to the knowledgeable Tiger, "went around Scotland for the king, getting the clans to become mates with William, but only the Campbell mob and a few others of their boot-lickers would have him on. Then King William got another Campbell, who was the Earl of Breadalbane, to go around hounding the clans, who had not sworn to support

William, to do so or get wiped out."

"Breadalbane," remarked Tiger, as Scotty paused for breath, "is a small hamlet about fifteen miles from Goulburn in New South Wales."

"Will you keep your mouth shut, you walking atlas?" roared Humpy, turning fiercely on Tiger. "One more word out of you and I'll drop you into the swamp. All right, Scotty, get a move on. This is hot stuff. I'm blessed if I knew that I had dukes and earls among my relations."

"A fine bunch they were," said Scotty. "Anyway, this Campbell—"

"Bloke from Breadalbane?" inquired Humpy.

"Yes. He managed to kid all the clans except the Macdonalds of Glencoe to sign up with King William. They all had to be in by New Year's Eve 1692. The Macdonald chief missed out, but he signed up a couple of days later. That didn't stop the Campbells, however. They were egged on by a toe-rag of a villain named Sir John Dalrymple. He and the Campbells fixed it to bump off all the Macdonalds no matter if they had signed the agreement to become King William's subjects. The king didn't care what they did. Campbell took half his clan and a big squad of soldiers into Glencoe and made friends with the people. They lived with them and when all was nice and quiet and friendly, they turned round and murdered the Macdonalds right and left. They flattened out over 120 men, women and little kids-just like you flattened out that reed warbler, Humpy."

"Whacko!" shouted Humpy. "The Campbells are coming, hurrah, hurrah!"

"Your mob," said Scotty darkly, "shot down little kids and cut off their poor little hands and ears, and chopped up old women and old men, burned down their houses, slaughtered them like anything. They did all this when the

Macdonalds were sleeping peacefully in their beds, early in the morning. They were all unarmed. They never had a chance. Just like that reed warbler, Humpy."

"Gee whizz!" breathed Humpy. "Cleaned out a whole town, huh?"

"Yeah! About a thousand Campbells and British soldiers and other riff-raff, all armed, killed about 200 harmless people. Oh, yes, nice carryings-on, I must say!"

"But tell me," said Humpy. "You mentioned some peanut named Dalrymple. Exactly where did he come into it?"

"He was in some job in England, licking the king's boots. I think he represented Scotland in the British Parliament. He was the joker who got King William to sign the order for the Campbell crowd to massacre the Macdonalds. He said we were just a lot of thieves," said Scotty moodily.

"Well, that was fair enough," grinned Humpy. "And how did he finish up?"

"The king made him the Earl of Stair," replied Scotty dolefully. "It seems to me that you Macdonald birds were as popular as an onion in a scent factory."

"But as all this happened so many years ago, does it really matter now?" Egghead wanted to know.

"Not a scrap," said Tiger. "But it does tend to show that what is bred in a Campbell stays there. I refer to the unnecessary and cowardly killing of an innocent reed warbler."

"Who's a coward?" demanded Humpy belligerently. "I can clean you up, any old tick of the clock. I'd have the three of you on if we were not in this punt."

"Any old excuse is better than none, you crooked-mouthed coot!" exclaimed Scotty.

"Eh? What brought that on?" ejaculated Humpy, rather taken aback. "Who says I'm crooked-mouthed? You must be nuts."

"All the Campbells are wry-mouthed. That is what Campbell means in Gaelic. Cameron means 'wry-nosed.' Macdonald, on the other hand, means 'world ruler.' Laugh that off, warbler-killer!"

"Listen to me, Scotty, I've just about had you. Punt or no punt, somebody else is going to have a crooked mouth and right now," howled the much-maligned Mr. Campbell. Saying which, he hurled himself upon his tormentor, and wrestled with him in the bottom of the punt, while Egghead and Tiger endeavoured to get out of the way.

There was insufficient room in the shallow-draught vessel for fighting, and both Egghead and Tiger were drawn willy-nilly into the affair. The punt was a quarter of a mile from the shore, and they could not reach dry land without wading or swimming through water, mud and reeds. They had, therefore, to put up with it or stop it.

"Pull them apart, Egghead," shouted Tiger, and then broke off with a grunt as Humpy's elbow caught him in the stomach. Humpy was now flat on his back on the bottom of the punt with Scotty astride him, but his flailing arms and legs prevented the onlookers from getting hold of him. Tiger grabbed Scotty round the waist and heaved, while Egghead, who was behind him, sought to help by winding his arms around Tiger's throat and heaving too.

"Stop that, Egghead!" gasped young Mr. Birch. "You're choking me." And when Egghead failed to desist, Tiger, in self-preservation, released his hold on Scotty and turned to grapple with the young migrant lad. While they were having their private brawl, Humpy succeeded in heaving Scotty off his chest and dragging himself to his feet, Scotty clinging to him. The two boys, their arms around each other, gasped and panted and uttered dire threats. Egghead, who was now crammed into the back of the punt with Tiger trying to choke him in retaliation, lashed out wildly with both fists and Tiger stopped one with his nose.

With a roar of pain, he jerked backwards, crashed into the struggling Scotty and Humpy, causing the punt to rock violently. Scotty and Humpy, still locked in their death struggle, toppled sideways. There were two loud howls and a mighty splashing sound as they vanished overboard into the murky waters of the swamp.

Egghead and Tiger grabbed the side of the punt to keep it from overturning, and watched Scotty and Humpy, wet and muddy, still struggling in the swamp, which, at that spot, was only two feet deep.

"Cut it out, you two, and get back into the punt," said Tiger.

"Not before I've Glen coed this Scotch coot," exclaimed Humpy as he made a wild swing at young Macdonald. It missed and he fell face downwards into the swamp again. Scotty grabbed the side of the punt and hauled himself aboard. Then, picking up the punt pole, he aimed it at Hum py like a spear.

"You can swim ashore, you useless warblerkiller ," he howled. "You're not coming back in this punt, no matter if your old man does own it. I'll teach you a lesson you won't forget in a hurry."

Humpy waded to the punt and got a poke in the chest. The things he said to and about Scotty were not only deplorable but, for the most part, quite inaccurate.

"I came out here in this punt and I'm going back in it," he said between his teeth. "If I don't, none of you coves do. I'll sink it first."

"Stop accing the goat, Scotty," said Tiger Birch. "You and Humpy are both wet through and you'll get pneumonia if you don't go and get changed. Remember, Humpy's old man doesn't know that we have the punt. If he finds out, we'll never get it again and Humpy will get a belting."

"A fat lot I care about that."

"Maybe not. But if his old man tells our old men, we'll all get a hiding. What about that?" Scotty thought that over for a few seconds and then eyed Humpy balefully.

"All right," he said. "We declare a truce for the time being. Humpy can come into the punt and we'll say no more about it just now. But no funny business, Humpy."

The wet and shivering Humpy clambered on board and Scotty surrendered the pole to him. Dead silence reigned as they made their way slowly back to the shore and tied the punt up to the ramshackle pier that Mr. Campbell had built for it. They were all standing on this shaky landing, their backs towards the farm, when a stentorian voice hailed them:—

"What the devil do you kids think you are doing?" It was Mr. Campbell! He marched up to them and eyed them sternly.

"We weren't going out in the punt, dad," said Humpy quickly. "We were just looking it over."

"Seeing that you just brought it in and I saw you do it, I guess you were not planning to sail it," his father replied. "What is the meaning of this? Didn't I tell you never to take the punt out without permission? And look at your clothes. Have you been swimming in them?"

"No, I fell overboard," muttered Humpy. "And I suppose young Macdonald here dived overboard and rescued you?" snorted Mr. Campbell, pointing at Scotty.

"That's right, Mr. Campbell," said Scotty calmly. "I'm a bit of a hero. He would have drowned only I plunged in and pulled him out."

"Why, you—you—you..." spluttered Humpy, words

failing him. Egghead and Tiger looked at Scotty in awe-stricken amazement.

"I don't believe a word of anything that has been said so far," said Mr. Campbell. "Here, you, whatever your name is, you tell me what happened. And I want the truth, see?"

He glared at Egghead, who looked vague. "Thank you very much, sir," he said obscurely. "I must be going now. My parents will be worried if I am late. Pleased to meet you, sir. I do not talk English very well. Please excuse me." Bowing gracefully like a Chinese mandarin as he stepped slowly backwards, Egghead suddenly whirled around and took to his heels like a startled rabbit.

"Wait for me, Egghead," shouted Tiger, and took after him like a second startled rabbit.

Mr. Campbell watched these proceedings in amazement.

"We'll go into all this later, Jimmy," he informed his son. "You'd better get up to the house and change your clothes before you catch a cold. That applies to you also, young Macdonald. And in future, don't come around here encouraging my poor silly son to go out on that swamp in my punt."

"I didn't encourage the goat," exclaimed Scotty. "He doesn't need any encouragement to act the nanny."

"Buzz off home before I take off my belt and lam you like I'm going to lam this bright lad," said Mr. Campbell.

Scotty walked away with great dignity, but when he reached what he judged to be a safe distance, he turned round and shouted, "Remember Glencoe!" Having delivered this parting shot, he took to his heels.

"What was that he sang out? Something about his Uncle Joe?" Mr. Campbell asked his gloomy son.

"Dunno," grunted Humpy impolitely.

"Well, get off home," said his father. "I want to have a

look at this punt to see what damage you have done to it."

Without a word, the wet, bedraggled and shivering Humpy squelched his way across the paddock. Nearing the fence which divided the lucerne patch from the paddock, he noticed the old family cow peacefully grazing. On her back rode Willy Wagtail. The little busybody stood on the cow's backbone, legs astride, huge tail swaying from side to side.

"Sweet pretty creature," he greeted Humpy.

"Shut up," said that lad ungraciously, and Willy made a noise like somebody shaking half a dozen loose matches in a box.

"Are you the same black-and-white mug that is always getting in my hair?" snorted the boy.

"Did-ja-did-ja-did-ja-did!"

"Are you any relation to that waggi my cat nearly got a couple of weeks ago? Or that other one who helped to push me into the creek? If so, I'll flatten you," said Humpy.

Instead of replying, Willy darted into the air after a small beetle, hounded it to earth, seized it in his beak, returned to the cow's back and calmly swallowed his prize.

"Hope it gives you the tummyache," said Humpy vindictively.

"Sweet pretty creature," sneered Willy.

Stooping down, Humpy picked up a stone and hurled it at Willy. The stone struck the old cow in the ribs. She mooed her surprise and lumbered away, Willy still clinging to her back. A second stone whizzed past, scaring Willy, who took to the air and streaked away across the paddock.

Willy did not stop until he reached the willows; Jimmy did not stop until he reached home; and when his mother saw his dirty, wet appearance, she did not stop talking for five minutes.

CHAPTER SEVEN
WILLY'S BUSY DAY

RUNNING and hopping around an open patch of grassland along the bank of the creek not far from their willow tree, Willy Wagtail and his mate were busily engaged in getting their breakfasts. Their family, the whole three of them, had been launched into the world and very shortly they would be thinking about rearing another brood. Like many other small birds, the wagtails did not always use the same nest for successive families, but sometimes built a new home if they needed it. Their friends the peewits were different. They cleaned out and relined their old nest, seeing no sense in working when it could be avoided. The peewits had had only two youngsters. Four eggs had been laid, but only two had hatched. The third had been addled, while the fourth had come to a violent end in the mouth of Tiger Birch as already related. It was perhaps the thought that he might soon be engaged again in the tiresome business of collecting strips of bark, cowhair, spider webs and other material and welding it into a cup-shaped receptacle, that prompted Willy to go exploring along the creek. There would be scant time for touring when Nature blew her whistle for the nest-erection shift to commence.

Leaving his small mate busily catching insects, Willy darted off along the creek bank, alighting in a stunted acacia bush. Using this as a temporary base from which to make air sallies after winged food, he next proceeded to the lowest branch of a gnarled and twisted old tree that hung over the water. Swaying gently to and fro, he surveyed the scenery on the other side of the creek and was delighted to observe a number of small creatures disporting themselves in the water. He was delighted because here was something into which he could stick his inquisitive and uninvited beak.

The object of his approving gaze was a family of water rats. There were the parents and two young ones. About six feet out from the bank a large flat rock stood a few inches clear of the surface, and the pretty little golden-brown creatures, their rich seal-like fur glittering wetly in the bright morning sun, were engaged in diving in and out of the stream, hunting for their food.

These water rats lived on yabbies, fish and snails and, if they could get them, small birds and their eggs. They dwelt in a long burrow they had driven into the creek bank. It went straight in for a foot or so and then turned, running parallel with the creek for fully fifteen feet and inclining upwards. This ensured that in flood time the water could not reach the nesting chamber which was established at the end of the tunnel. It was a fairly large space, hollowed out and filled cosily with bark, twigs and dried grass. Near this nesting chamber they had constructed a second one which they used as a storeroom. From this storeroom another and smaller tunnel ran upwards, opening near a tuft of thick, coarse grass, which effectually screened it. This shaft provided ventilation for the whole burrow, as well as an escape route if needed.

The water rats did not take their meals into their burrow, but used the flat stone surrounded by water as both a dining table and a diving platform, shooting off it into the stream and bringing back any food they caught, to be shared by all.

And as Willy Wagtail watched them, he saw one of the parents emerge dripping from the water with a wriggling yabbie in his mouth. The freshwater crayfish was endeavouring to seize its captor with its sharp claws, but the rat held it in such a way that it could not reach back far enough to get a grip. One vicious bite of the rat's teeth soon put an end to the yabbie's struggles and soon the rat family was disposing of the succulent flesh, ripping it from the hard shell and discarding the remnants by flicking them into the stream.

Flitting across the creek, Willy made a dive at the flat rock and the feasting rats, letting out a stream of harsh chatter like a feathered machinegun. The furred family did not stop to ask questions, but dived into the creek in a body. This pleased Willy immensely. He alighted on the rock, cackling to himself with brazen self-congratulation, and inspected the remains of the yabbie. There were shreds of flesh on the rock, and he gobbled up some of it. He found it to his taste, so had some more. It was the first time he had tried raw yabbie.

No doubt the wagtail would have gone on and eaten all the bits he could find—and probably made himself sick on such unfamiliar food—but he was interrupted.

Pecking around, he was suddenly startled to find himself staring into a couple of bright little eyes behind a pointed whiskery nose. Father Water Rat was in the act of climbing back on to the stone.

"Did-ja-did-ja-did-ja-did!" squawked Willy, trying to intimidate the rat, who stared at him with unblinking eyes.

Willy's surprise was even greater when he felt a sudden

tug at his tail. Swivelling around, he found himself gazing into another pair of bright eyes behind a pointed, whiskery nose. One of the young rats had come out of the water behind him and had made a grab at Willy's most prominent feature.

With a frightened chirp, the wagtail leaped straight into the air and darted wildly back to the old gnarled tree across the creek. It had been a narrow escape, for, had he stayed any longer on that rock, the water rat family undoubtedly would have had him for dessert. If Willy never before had tasted yabbie, the rats never before had tasted wagtail, but they had been more than ready to embark upon the experiment.

Willy, feeling flustered, perched in the old tree and when his heart had resumed its regular beating, he flew off to a tall red gum some distance from the creek bank. The first thing he noticed when he alighted was a large mud nest built on a thick limb. It was much larger than any built by his friends the peewits.

Having ascertained by a careful look around that there were no birds nearby, Willy perched on the edge of the nest and inspected it. The nest was about two feet in circumference, nine inches across and six inches deep, and it contained nine yellow-white, brown-blotched eggs nestling in a lining of dried grass and bits of fur.

The nest was the property of a community of white-winged choughs or black magpies. These large black birds were as clannish as young Scotty Macdonald. They lived together in flocks and when breeding time came around, they all pitched in and helped in nest-building like a gang of human carpenters erecting a house. When a nest was completed, two hens sometimes would share it.

These choughs were almost ready to begin incubating their eggs and the main reason the birds were not at the nest just then was that, like the peewits, they spent more time on the ground than in the trees or the air. In dress the choughs might resemble a flock of bush undertakers looking for a funeral, but actually they were a frolicsome lot. One of their chief pastimes was playing "follow-the-leader" and while Willy Wagtail was inspecting the nest, a dozen of them were playing it some distance off.

It was when they neared the tree in which the nest stood that Willy Wagtail saw them, and should have taken himself off, because their affairs had nothing to do with him. But that was the reason he stayed.

Perched on the branch by the nest, he peered downwards as a series of harsh cries floated through the trees. As he watched, he saw one chough pick up a dead twig and wave it with his beak. Immediately, another chough grabbed the other end and they indulged in a miniature tug-of-war for a few moments. It ended when one bird let go suddenly. Its friend fell backwards and began to squawk like a nestling. This caused the rest of the flock to hurry to its side, gather in a circle around it, and act as if they were feeding it. Tiring of this sport, one chough ran along the ground chirping. His companions at once followed him in single file until they reached the foot of the nest tree. The leading bird flew up on to a low branch, ran along it a few feet, and then dropped down on the other side to the ground. The whole string of choughs faithfully followed him. Around the tree trunk in a circle they raced in single file, and up, along and over the branch to the ground, again and again.

Willy Wagtail, never a grandstand player or armchair critic, decided to join in the game and his participation was, to say the least, rather unorthodox. He did not join in the queue and become a small link in the "follow-the-leader" chain. Not he! He waited until the flock reached the ground after going over the branch for perhaps the fifteenth time and then he darted off his branch and launched an attack on the leading bird, pecking it on the back of the head and, darting to the rear, did likewise to the tail-ender. Up and down the line he went, pecking and chattering. This thoroughly disorganised the game, which pleased him immensely. The flock of choughs said things about him that would have wounded the feelings of any sensitive bird.

Leaving the disgruntled choughs to sort themselves out, Willy flew back to the nest, perched on the rim of it and eyed the eggs pensively. His inspection lasted two seconds. The two female choughs who were sharing the nest came at him savagely and from opposite directions. Willy saw them a split second before their sharp beaks could mess up his feathers and he leaped into the air with a startled chirp. The avenging choughs collided violently right over the nest and fell into it, fighting each other savagely. Willy did not stay to apologise, but streaked away, the wits scared out of him. He shot into a red gum and nestled among the leaves, hoping that the irate choughs would not discover him. He had no need to worry about that. The big black birds were fighting among themselves and had no time to spare thinking about him.

As he sat quietly on a twig, getting his breath back, Willy heard faint chirping noises nearby. He looked around inquiringly and found that he had landed quite near the nest of a brown weebill or tree-tit. It was a small, globular erection with a door near the top like a spout, made of grass tied together with spider webs. The chirpings came from the nest and he knew that they were made by nestlings.

Still shaken by his encounter with the choughs, Willy decided not to interfere with this nest. He had had enough of nests for the time being and did not want any trouble with anyone. He was about to take off and fly back along the creek towards his own home when a very small brown bird popped out of the weebill's nest right on top of him. Willy himself was no feathered giant, but he made three of this tiny tree-tit. But, small as it was, it demonstrated that it had absolutely no use for Willy.

"Winnie-wieldt! Winnie-wieldt!" it shrilled at him, telling him plainly to clear out. Willy was in no mood for cheek from tiny weebills. He pivoted in a half-circle and his huge tail swept the tree-tit off the twig on which it perched. With a startled twitter, it fluttered up to its nest and dived down the spout for safety. Willy, his self-esteem partly restored, flew off along the creek and into more trouble.

He became aware that something was up as he neared his willow. Loud calls of "ya-hoo! ya-hoo! ya-hoo!" informed him that he had visitors and that these visitors, pests like himself, were having fun and games.

He landed in his willow on a branch well away from his nest, and rage filled him when he saw what was going on. A pair of grey-crowned babblers or apostle-birds were up to their old games. They had torn his nest to bits and were even now squabbling over the last pieces. Willy and his mate had intended to build a new nest, but that was beside the point. These pests, these babblers, these apostle-birds, these chatterers, these cacklers, these barkers, these pine-birds, these catbirds, these dog-birds, codlin-moth-eaters, hoppers, jumpers, yahoos, happy families, happy jacks, twelve apostles, parson birds-oh, they had a host of names-couldn't get away with this! They thought they were smart, going around the bush tearing to pieces the nests of other birds. They were always at it! It would be bad enough if they took away the material from destroyed nests to build homes of their own, but they didn't. They just threw it away. Generally they got around in parties of up to a dozen, hence their name "Twelve Apostles." Thank goodness, there were only two of them here!

Willy charged them like a bull at a gate, "did-jadid-ja-diddering" with all his might. He clung to the back of one of them, pecking its head madly. The surprised apostle flapped its wings and shook its head, but could not dislodge the wagtail. Its mate did that. It lunged at Willy with its long, sharp beak, poking him savagely in the ribs. Willy released his hold and took to the air, while the apostles both flew down to the ground and started searching for insects as if nothing had happened.

Willy was prepared to have another go at them, but changed his mind when he saw the remains of his nest. He was chattering his rage to high heaven when his mate joined him and added her chatter to his. Calming down eventually, Willy began to wonder why his friends the peewits had not interfered with the playful apostles. Spiralling upwards, Willy flew to where the peewits' mud nest rested. Those birds had been preparing for their second clutch of eggs.

And what Willy found there was the last, the definitely final, straw. The peewits' nest was still there and intact, but it was occupied by a whitebreasted wood swallow, who looked at him benevolently. It had no quarrel with the wagtail.

The wood swallow and its mate had not long arrived in the district. They were migrants, wintering in the far north and returning to the south to breed in the springtime. The fact that the wood swallow was a beautiful-looking bird, graceful in flight and friendly in habits, did not impress Willy Wagtail. Where were his peewit friends? They would not have given up their nest without a fight, neither would the wood swallow have sought to take violent possession of it. That was not the disposition of the bird. Its natural nest was a cup-shaped one of dried grass built in the fork of a tree, or in a hollow limb; but it was quite common for wood swallows to take over the nests of peewits when the owners had quite finished with them. Maybe the pair of yahoos who had destroyed his own nest had hunted the peewits away, and the newly arrived wood swallow had taken advantage of the situation.

Willy did not know the answer to all these questions. All he knew was that the peewits had gone, and so was his own nest. Being a wagtail, he would not think of nesting except in the company of a peewit. There was, therefore, no future for him and his mate in this particular willow tree.

That night the two wagtails roosted in a grey gum half a mile up the creek. It had been a crowded day for Willy, and he was glad to turn in.

CHAPTER EIGHT
UNCLE JIM

WHEN Scotty Macdonald's Uncle Jim Thomas arrived in his utility truck and caravan for a holiday, Scotty and his mates were highly delighted. They did not approve of many of their relations, but they did approve of genial Jim Thomas. He was a friendly soul who understood youngsters and got on well with them. There were some folks who said that Uncle Jim was "queer" because he did not always conform to the rigid discipline of polite society. He was an individualist, who preferred a roving life, did as he liked, and was in the position financially to do so. Uncle Jim's idea of visiting his sister Jean and her husband, Angus Macdonald, parents of Scotty, was to look in on them at their farmhouse, give them a cheery "Hullo" and then take his caravan to the bank of that portion of the creek that ran through their property. He said he was used to the great open spaces. He had knocked about all over Australia and was quite happy with the life of a rolling stone without a wife or family. He said he felt as if he were in gaol living in a house filled with people; so if the Macdonalds did not mind, he would camp down on the creek bank and look them up from time to time.

It was a glorious moonlight night, with the soft lunar

radiance bathing the creek, the farms and the bush beyond in a mantle of molten silver. Uncle Jim had built a cheery campfire and, with pipe in mouth, was entertaining Scotty, Tiger and Egghead with tales of travel in distant places. When the lads had arrived not long after tea, he had noted the absence of Humpy, but had not commented upon it.

"Been around much, Uncle Jim, since you were here two years ago?" asked Scotty.

"Yes," he replied. "I had a bit of a tour through western Queensland, across the South Australian border and finished up at Alice Springs. Then I went down to Adelaide, where I stayed a while, and then gradually made my way back here.

"Incidentally, while I was in Adelaide, I added to my store of bush knowledge. I met a man who was connected with the production and collection of pine seed. He told me that on his plantation they let the black cockatoos do all the work."

"In what way?" inquired Tiger Birch.

"Well, these black cockatoos love pine seeds, but they only take a few from each cone, before knocking the cone off the tree. Men used to be employed ciimbing the pine trees and knocking the cones down to be collected by other men. But when it was discovered that the cockatoos only succeeded in getting a few seeds before their attacks on the cones knocked them off the trees, the men stopped the hard work of climbing the trees and just let the cockies do the work. They found, too, that the black cockatoos knew better than they did which cones contained the ripe seeds. Now, they just go around the pine forest with bags and pick up all the cones they need without having to climb for them. Before they found all this out, the men had tried to get rid of the black cockies, thinking that they ate too many of the seeds and were prize pests."

"Well, what do you know about that!" said Scotty, in admiration of human ingenuity and cockatoo lack of it.

"Did you have any exciting adventures while you were travelling around, Uncle Jim?" inquired Egghead.

"None at all," drawled Uncle Jim.

"Ja-did-ja-did-ja-did!" came a sudden voice from the willow top. Uncle Jim burst into a chuckle.

"Willy Wagtail is making a liar out of me," he grinned. "It's a fact, Willy!" he shouted. "There was nothing out of the box this trip."

"What's that silly little coot doing singing out at this time of night?" snorted Scotty. "If I had my catapult here, I'd give him something to go on with."

"I'll give you a smart lift under the ear, Scotty, if I ever catch you shooting any of the bush birds, and especially Willy Wagtail," said Uncle Jim sternly. "As for him calling out, wagtails often do on moonlight nights. Willy has a nest up in that willow and he is warning us to keep away from it. I met Willy today. I had no sooner poked my nose out of the caravan first thing this morning than he was hopping around the place and 'sweet pretty creaturing' me for all he was worth. He didn't stay long because, as I said, he has a nest in the willows and there are young ones in it. He and his mate have been feeding them all day long.

"There was a bit of excitement this afternoon," he went on, with a chuckle. "Old Jack Kookaburra came along. He first perched in that gum tree over there. I thought he was visiting me, but he had his eye on Willy's nestlings, for sure. Or it might have been the peewits who have a nest in the same willow. Anyhow, Willy saw Old Jack in the gum tree, and you should have heard his language! This brought the peewits along, and the three of them abused that bird like nobody's business. They flew at him and pecked at him until it got on his nerves and he flew away. If he hadn't, I would have hunted him. Willy is a pal of mine and I won't have any kookaburras stealing his youngsters. I'll stay here until they are big enough to leave the nest, in case Old Jack should be back. He probably won't, with me around."

"But don't you think Willy is a bit of a dill, singing out at night?" asked Scotty. "He'd have more sense if he kept quiet. Yelling out is just inviting the owls and the rest of them to come around. If he kept his beak shut, they wouldn't know he had a nest there. He's balmy."

"Balmy or not, I've got a lot of time for Willy Wagtail," said Uncle Jim. "He is such an amiable and friendly little chap, and as brave as they make 'em. Many's the time I've only had a wagtail for company in the lonely bush. There have been occasions when I've been camping hundreds of miles away from the nearest human settlement and Willy Wagtail has been the only creature to be chummy. He'd come around the camp and chatter away as friendly as anything. The rest of the birds always gave me a wide berth—as if I'd hurt any of them! I tell you, lads, that little black-and-white fellow has more human friends than all the rest of the bush birds put together. Willy is chummy with everyone, even the most disreputable and destitute swaggie or dead-beat sundowner. The lonely man on the track, without human friends, will not have one bad word said about Willy Wagtail, and don't you forget it."

"After all, it is just sheer inquisitiveness on Willy's part," observed Tiger Birch. "I like him a lot, but he is definitely a stickybeak."

"Possibly," retorted Uncle Jim, "but you'll never convince a swaggie of that."

"By the way, Uncle Jim, here is something you might be able to tell me, as you've been all over Australia," said

Tiger. "Why do wagtails always make their nests in the same tree as mudlarks?"

"Not always, Tiger. On many occasions, you will find mudlarks, or peewits, nesting in the same tree as Willy Wagtail's relation, the restless flycatcher, or scissors grinder as some call him. He looks a lot like Willy, who, actually, is a black-and-white fantail. Again, you will find grinders and waggies nesting together, and sometimes the whole three-mudlarks, waggies and grinders. But, as you say, wagtails and mudlarks are found together in ninety-nine cases out of a hundred. As to why they do this, I do not know. You can buy into plenty of arguments about that. Some say that it is because the birds are all black-and-white; others have it that it is for self-protection. Personally, I haven't a clue."

"There is a peewit's nest in a willow along the creek not far from here," commented Scotty, and broke off suddenly with a yelp as Tiger kicked him in the shin.

"What the heck was that in aid of, Tiger?" he yelled, rubbing his leg.

"Keep your mouth shut about that peewit's nest!" hissed Tiger.

"Oh, I'm a wake-up!" said Scotty with a grin. "I wasn't going to say anything about Humpy dropping that egg into your beak. It was something else."

"Big mouth," growled Tiger. "You've already said it." Uncle Jim inquired what all the grinning and growling was about, and when told of the episode of the peewit's egg, he laughed heartily, much to Tiger's chagrin.

"What I was going to say," chuckled Scotty, "was that the other day I was along the creek and saw a wood swallow sitting in the peewit's nest. There was no sign of the peewit."

"Wood swallows often steal peewits' nests," said Uncle Jim. "Many other birds do, too. Peewits' nests seem to have some fatal attraction. I've seen blackfaced cuckoo-shrikes, or leatherheads, apostle birds and babblers nesting in them. A friend of mine swears, too, that he once saw a wagtail using one. Anyway, nest-stealing is very common. There are hundreds of instances of it.

"And, talking about mudlarks, or peewits, or what have you," he continued, "I had a very interesting experience with some of them last summer. I never felt so sorry for anyone as I did for those poor old birds."

"Did you kill them?" inquired Scotty.

"No, I didn't kill them!" exclaimed Uncle Jim. "That is all some of you lads seem to think about! But old Mother Nature nearly killed them. It was a scurvy trick she played on them.

"It was like this. I was camping for a few days along a bit of a creek that had nearly dried up. It was a very hot, dry season, as you know. This creek had a hard rocky bottom and sandy edges. The drought had dried up every waterhole for miles, and the peewits couldn't find any mud to build their nests. I was so interested in their efforts that I stayed there longer than I had intended.

"One pair I had my eye on had started a nest, but had run out of mud and were at their wits' end. There was none around the sandy, rocky creek, so I tried an experiment. I got a bucket of water and emptied it over the ground some distance from the creek bank. Believe me, those peewits tore into it as if their very lives depended on it. The weather was so hot that the mud patch kept drying out.

"In the end, I dug a hole and filled it with hard bits of stone well stamped down. I filled this with water, and, bless me, peewits, swallows, choughs and apostle birds—the only four kinds in Australia who build mud nests—seemed to come from everywhere. They grabbed beakfuls of mud and moved to and fro like jet planes. Anyway, I couldn't stay there for the rest of my life. I had to push on. I came back that way a week later, and I had no sooner made my appearance than all the swallows, peewits and choughs and apostles were around me, or rather around the dried-up well I had made. They all wanted to finish their nests and were depending upon me to supply the mud. It was all right while only a few birds were wanting supplies, but I couldn't stay there indefinitely making mudpies for hundreds!

"One day I decided that, come what may, I was leaving next morning. That night it started to rain and it rained heavily for two solid days. The local mud-nesters were saved."

Dead silence greeted Uncle Jim as he finished his story, and then, apropos of nothing, Egghead remarked, "Quite so."

"It's lovely in the moonlight," commented Scotty.

"Yes, Tiger?" asked Uncle Jim gently. "Your comments, please? I'm a thundering liar, aren't I? You might as well be in it."

"I don't think so," said Tiger. "I read in a magazine not long ago about the drought being so severe one year that birds who built mud nests had had to delay their nesting season because of the mud shortage. These birds, the book said, did not get enough material until nearly winter, with the result that when their young ones hatched, a lot of them died through the cold weather. The birds had been forced to nest out of season."

"I didn't say you were a liar, Uncle Jim," protested Scotty.

"No, but you thought it, didn't you?" retorted his uncle. "You want to wake up to yourself, boy, and to the fact that birds are most unpredictable. Nobody can say what they are likely to do and what is likely to alter their mode of life. It is the same with human beings. Never forget that, in life, everyone's normal routine and habits are subject to disarrangement by circumstances."

"Yes, uncle," said Scotty. "And that goes for you, too, young Egghead."

"Yes," said the bearer of that undistinguished nickname, wondering why Scotty had picked on him.

"There is another side to the drought story," said Uncle Jim. "It often happens that after a long, dry season, during which birds cannot breed as much as usual, a bountiful period of good rains follows, and the birds make up for it by breeding prolifically. That is when a lot of nest-stealing goes on, especially among the birds that build in small shrubs and tall grass."

"I've often seen sparrows in bottle swallows' nests," said Scotty. "They wait until the swallow is about to add the spout and then hop in and take over before the spout is built."

"I have been told that the cuckoos steal the nests of all the birds," said Egghead.

"Then you have been told wrongly," said Uncle Jim. "Cuckoos neither build nests nor steal them. They lay their eggs in the nests of other birds and expect those birds to rear their young."

"Yes, that is so," said Tiger. "The other week I found a cuckoo's egg in a tom-tit's nest and I smashed the thing against the side of the tree. That is one less cuckoo. I never kill the bush birds, but I'm right up against cuckoos. I reckon they have a hide expecting other birds to rear their young ones for them. If that egg had hatched, the young cuckoo would have slung the little tom-tits out and had the nest and all the tucker to himself. It ain't right and it ain't a fair go."

"H'm. I don't know that you acted rightly," mused Uncle Jim. "It's a hard question to decide. As you say, the tom-tits—by which I take it you mean yellow-tailed thornbills, would have reared up a batch of young ones if the cuckoo's egg had not been deposited in their nest. Had the young cuckoo been hatched out, it certainly would have tossed the young thornbills from the nest. As I say, it is a tough problem. The thornbills owned the nest and their young ones had prior right of survival. On the other hand, you cannot blame the cuckoo. It was created by Nature just the same as the thorn bills, and Nature, for some reason, decreed that it should not build a nest of its own, but should use that of some other bird."

"Then what would you do if you found a cuckoo's egg in a nest, Uncle Jim?" asked Egghead, who had followed the conversation with deep interest. "Would you throw it out?"

"I don't know," said Jim frankly. "It probably would depend upon the mood I was in at the time. Taking it by and large, we must assume that Nature knows what she is doing and we should not interfere."

"And let a lot of dashed innocent birds suffer?" cried Scotty indignantly. "I'd do what Tiger did and sling the dashed cuckoo's egg at the nearest tree."

"You forget that the baby cuckoo is also a little innocent bird, with as much right to live as any of the other bush birds," said Uncle Jim.

"Yes, but at the expense of several others," said Tiger.

"Tiger, my lad," said Jim Thomas gently, "Nature's first law is that the weak shall go under in order that the strong may survive. And remember, the cuckoo lays only one egg in a nest. It is far out-numbered by every other species of bird in the bush. It is also a most useful insect-eating bird."

"I stick to my own idea," said Tiger stubbornly.

"And I'm with you all the way," voted Scotty.

"I think that what Uncle Jim says is correct," said Egghead. "Do not interfere with the ways of Nature and her creatures."

"Two-all," smiled Jim Thomas. "Then we'll call it a draw and agree to differ, huh?"

Laughingly, they all agreed that that would be best.

"Anyway, if Humpy had been here, he would have voted with Scotty and me and we would have won," said Tiger. "Humpy would be in any violence."

"Incidentally," said Uncle Jim, "it is none of my business, but what caused the brawl between you three and young Campbell? I know there has been a brawl or he would have been with you tonight."

"The brawl was between me and Humpy," said Scotty. "Tiger and Egghead didn't come into it as much as I did. We had a general row with him about shooting a warbler with a catapult. Sheer murder it was."

"Was that all it was over?"

"No," said Scotty dramatically. "Remember Glencoe!"

"Remember who?" inquired Uncle Jim.

"Scotty called Humpy a murderer," said Tiger. "He said that Humpy murdered the reed warbler like the Campbell clan murdered the Macdonalds at Glencoe way back in the year dot."

"So he did!" snorted Scotty.

"You've been delving back into ancient history, huh?" smiled Jim Thomas. "You want to forget about all that. The Campbells are as good as any other Scots—better than a lot, in fact. One of my best friends is a Campbell and he wouldn't know a set of bagpipes if he tripped over them."

"What?" ejaculated Scotty, aghast. "How can you say such a thing? After what they did to us Macdonalds! Uncle Jim, you're a Scot yourself!"

"I am Australian, " said Uncle Jim. "My ancestors were Scots the same as yours, your father's and your mother's.

Be proud of it, but be proud that you're an Australian, too. Anyway, I'm afraid you are in for a bit of a shock, my lad. If you have been studying the histories of the Scottish clans, you have been a bit one-eyed in your studies; or at least you have concentrated upon the Macdonalds. Don't go around knocking the Campbells, my lad, because you're a sort of half a one yourself!"

"Hey?" roared Scotty, outraged. "Never in this life! How do you work that out?"

"Well, it's this way, Scotty. Your mother is my sister, therefore her maiden name was Thomas, which is a good Scots name. But the Thomases were never a separate clan, but a sept, or branch, or adherent, of another clan. Guess which one?"

"Macdonald of the Isles," said Scotty proudly.

"Campbell of Argyll," said Uncle Jim gently.

"Wh-a-a-a-t!" exclaimed Scotty passionately. "I don't believe it! It couldn't happen to me! It ain't true!"

"Go home and study your clan book carefully. You'll see," said Jim Thomas. "But why trouble? Why not have a bit of sense and forget all about it? We are all Australians here, you, Humpy, Tiger, me and even young Egghead."

"I am very proud that you should say so," said Egghead. "I am proud to be called Australian, and so are my mother and father, though they be from Poland."

"Me too," said Tiger, stoutly, if ungrammatically.

"Come to that, so am I," put in the still somewhat-dazed Scotty. "Half Macdonald, half Thomas, a bit of Campbell, but all Australian. What you might call a Scotch mixture."

There was silence for a few moments after that. The old creek shone silver in the moonlight, the campfire flickered and Uncle Jim's caravan gleamed pale against the dark willows. There was enchantment in the cool, sweet air. Down in the creek the frogs were croaking and from far away across the swamp there came the booming of a bittern.

"You know, boys," said Uncle Jim dreamily, "this is a grand country. I know that has been said by many people many times, but the fact remains so. I have been all over it. I've seen its great cities, its mighty industries, and its wonderful resources. I've travelled its vast plains, climbed its rugged ranges, wandered through its peaceful bushlands and dreamed by its quiet creeks and rivers. I've seen mighty floods devastate it and I've seen terrible bushfires ravish it."

He paused, and there was a faraway look in his eyes.

"Our ancestors came from far countries to open up Australia," he went on. "When one roams, as I have done, in the quiet of the bush, surrounded by the magnificent samples of Nature's handiwork—the great gums, the graceful wattle, the hardy spinifex; the many wonderful birds and animals, the like of which are to be found nowhere else in the world, I thank God for the heritage He has bestowed on Australians."

Uncle Jim looked steadily at the three rapt faces before him.

"It is up to you lads to carry on and to hold this country and everything it contains. You are Australians. Once again I say to you, be proud of that fact. There are no finer people in the world."

"Did-ja-did-ja-did!" came a voice from the willow top, as if in endorsement of what Jim Thomas had said.

"You, too, Willy Wagtail," said Uncle Jim soberly. "You are more truly an Australian than any of us. You can trace your Australian lineage right back through the centuries. We are, by comparison, merely newcomers." He smiled at Egghead. "New Australians. That is what we all are to Willy, you know."

"Sweet pretty creature," said the voice in the willows, softly and friendly.

"Thank you, Willy Wagtail," said Uncle Jim.

FINIS

www.ingramcontent.com/pod-product-compliance
Lightning Source LLC
Chambersburg PA
CBHW072151020426
42334CB00018B/1961

* 9 7 8 0 6 4 8 1 0 4 8 9 6 *